MAXIMIZING PSYCHOTHERAPEUTIC GAINS AND PREVENTING RELAPSE IN EMOTIONALLY DISTRESSED CLIENTS

John W. Ludgate, PhD

Bristol Therapy Associates
Bristol, Tennessee

Professional Resource Press
Sarasota, Florida

Published by
Professional Resource Press
(An imprint of the Professional Resource Exchange, Inc.)
Post Office Box 15560
Sarasota, FL 34277-1560

To receive the latest catalog from Professional Resource Press, please call 1-941-366-7913, fax (941-366-7971), or write to the address above.

Printed in the United States of America
Copyright © 1995 by Professional Resource Exchange, Inc.
All rights reserved

Terry S. Proeger, PhD, served as Editorial Consultant for this book.

The copy editor for this book was David Anson, the managing editor was Debra Fink, the production coordinator was Laurie Girsch, and the cover designer was Bill Tabler.

Library of Congress Cataloging-in-Publication Data

Ludgate, John W. date.
    Maximizing psychotherapeutic gains and preventing relapse in
emotionally distressed clients / John W. Ludgate.
        p.   cm. -- (Practitioner's resource series)
    Includes bibliographical references.
    ISBN 1-56887-014-0 (pbk. : alk. paper)
    1. Cognitive therapy. 2. Depression, Mental--Relapse--Prevention.
3. Anxiety--Relapse--Prevention. I. Title. II. Series.
    [DNLM: 1. Cognitive Therapy--methods. 2. Depressive Disorder-
-therapy. 3. Anxiety Disorders--therapy. 4. Recurrence. WM
425.5.C6 L944m 1995]
RC489.C63L83 1995
616.89'142--dc20
DNLM/DLC
for Library of Congress   95-20029
                                                              CIP

ACKNOWLEDGEMENTS

The author would like to express his gratitude to the following people: Ivy Blackburn, for inspiring his initial interest in Cognitive Therapy; Tim Beck, for the consistent encouragement and stimulation he provided in the author's professional development; Judy Beck and Robin Jarrett, for helping to clarify and expand his ideas on maintenance and relapse-prevention; Daniel and Matthew Ludgate for their love and support; Victor and Irene Ludgate for guidance, nurturance, and for their faith in the author over many years; and Vannessa Carter-Whatley for her inspiration, encouragement, and invaluable friendship.

PREFACE TO THE SERIES

As a publisher of books, cassettes, and continuing education programs, the Professional Resource Press and Professional Resource Exchange, Inc. strive to provide mental health professionals with highly applied resources that can be used to enhance clinical skills and expand practical knowledge.

All titles in the *Practitioner's Resource Series* are designed to provide important new information on topics of vital concern to psychologists, clinical social workers, marriage and family therapists, psychiatrists, and other mental health professionals.

Although the focus and content of each book in this series will be quite different, there will be notable similarities:

1. Each title in the series will address a timely topic of critical clinical importance.
2. The target audience for each title will be practicing mental health professionals. Our authors were chosen for their ability to provide concrete "how-to-do-it" guidance to colleagues who are trying to increase their competence in dealing with complex clinical problems.
3. The information provided in these books will represent "state-of-the-art" information and techniques derived from both clinical experience and empirical research. Each of these guide books will include references and resources for

those who wish to pursue more advanced study of the discussed topic.

4. The authors will provide numerous case studies, specific recommendations for practice, and the types of "nitty-gritty" details that clinicians need before they can incorporate new concepts and procedures into their practices.

We feel that one of the unique assets of the Professional Resource Press is that all of its editorial decisions are made by mental health professionals. The publisher, all editorial consultants, and all reviewers are practicing psychologists, marriage and family therapists, clinical social workers, and psychiatrists.

If there are other topics you would like to see addressed in this series, please let me know.

Lawrence G. Ritt, Publisher

FOREWORD

This concise volume on relapse prevention offers clear clinical guidelines applicable to a spectrum of patients with psychological disorders. Informed both by research and considerable clinical experience, Dr. Ludgate has produced an important supplement to the cognitive therapy literature created by Dr. Aaron T. Beck and his colleagues. The thrust of this volume is the application of cognitive therapy principles beyond the therapy session itself, focusing on methods to enable patients to become their own therapists. The dual emphasis on helping patients recover from psychological disorders in as efficient and effective manner as possible and on helping them stay well has become increasingly important in this era of health care reform. Cognitive therapy is ideally suited to both these challenges as it is short-term, problem-solving oriented, and highly educative in nature.

Dr. Ludgate notes that relapse prevention does not start at the end of therapy. Rather, patients learn and practice skills from the very first session. He clearly articulates the steps the therapist takes to teach specific tools and to encourage their use, over-learning, and generalization to other problems and settings. An important component of relapse prevention is anticipating high-risk situations and developing "emergency plans" to help reduce the frequency, severity, and duration of setbacks. Interventions are also described for patients who struggle with the termination phase of therapy, and for those who do relapse after therapy is over.

Applicable to individual and group therapy in outpatient and inpatient settings, *Maximizing Psychotherapeutic Gains and Preventing Relapse in Emotionally Distressed Clients* offers practical, concrete methods to help patients get the most from therapy.

Judith S. Beck, PhD, Director
Beck Institute for Cognitive
Therapy and Research
June 5, 1995

ABSTRACT

Cognitive-behavioral methods have shown considerable promise both in promoting short-term improvement and in preventing relapse in emotionally distressed patients. There are, however, few comprehensive practical guidelines for the practitioner wishing to implement cognitive-behavioral strategies in an attempt to maximize therapeutic gains and prevent symptom recurrence in such patients. This book aims to fill the gap. It provides an overview of cognitive-behavior therapy and its relationship to maintenance and relapse. Relapse rates and predictors of relapse in the areas of depression and anxiety are reviewed. Practical procedures to facilitate maintenance and prevent relapse, which can be used at different points in therapy and in the after-care phase, are described in detail with several case examples. Specific difficulties encountered in working to maintain treatment gains and prevent relapse are outlined and possible solutions are explored. Finally, some general guidelines for therapists working with patients who have relapsed are offered.

TABLE OF CONTENTS

MAXIMIZING PSYCHOTHERAPEUTIC GAINS AND PREVENTING RELAPSE IN EMOTIONALLY DISTRESSED CLIENTS

OVERVIEW OF COGNITIVE-BEHAVIORAL THERAPY (CBT) AND RELAPSE

In the last two decades there has been a virtual explosion of interest in effective short-term psychotherapies for use with emotionally distressed clients. Of these therapy approaches, cognitive-behavioral methods have received considerable attention (especially in the areas of depression, anxiety, and other related disorders) due to their apparent promise in promoting maintenance of treatment gains and preventing relapse. This introductory section will review the goals and strategies of cognitive-behavioral therapy (CBT) and how these relate to the objectives of relapse-prevention.

Cognitive-behavioral approaches seem to have attracted clinicians from both behavioral and psychodynamic traditions. In fact, the theoretical basis of cognitive-behavioral therapy includes cognitive psychology (i.e., information processing and social psychology), as well as modern behaviorism and psychoanalysis. The principle theoretical assumptions of this model are

- Cognitions influence mood and behavior.

1

- Perceptions and cognitions mediate the effects of situations on mood and behavior.
- Cognition includes automatic thoughts, images, beliefs, underlying assumptions, and memories.
- Different emotional disorders have distinct cognitive themes (i.e., specific automatic thoughts and beliefs).
- In disorders of mood and behavior there are often underlying information-processing deficits or cognitive distortions.
- Underlying thoughts and beliefs are often acquired as a result of early experience.
- Modification of cognitions leads to emotional and behavioral change.

The goals of cognitive-behavioral therapy with emotional disorders are (a) to reduce depressive and anxious symptoms, (b) to help the patient develop self-management skills, and (c) to promote maintenance of treatment gains and facilitate relapse-prevention.

These goals will be accomplished by the following means:

- identifying and challenging negative thoughts and maladaptive beliefs
- helping the patient develop more adaptive beliefs and attitudes
- getting the patient to practice and rehearse new cognitive and behavioral responses

Specific procedures and strategies for accomplishing these objectives with depressed and anxious clients are well documented in A. T. Beck et al. (1979) and A. T. Beck and Emery (1985). The principle characteristics of the practice of cognitive therapy as outlined by A. T. Beck and Emery (1985) are as follows:

1. Cognitive therapy is based on a cognitive model of emotional disorders.
2. Cognitive therapy is brief and time limited.
3. A sound therapeutic relationship is a necessary condition for effective cognitive therapy.

4. Cognitive therapy is a collaborative effort between thera-pist and patient.
5. Cognitive therapy uses primarily a Socratic method of questioning.
6. Cognitive therapy is structured and directive.
7. Cognitive therapy is problem oriented and focused on the here-and-now.
8. Cognitive therapy is based on an educational model.
9. The theory and techniques of cognitive therapy rely on the inductive method (i.e., guided discovery).
10. Homework is a central feature of cognitive therapy.

In actual clinical practice, the cognitive-behavioral therapist may employ a variety of cognitive and behavioral techniques to alter the dysfunctional cognitions and behaviors that contribute to a patient's emotional distress. Cognitive techniques may include (a) identifying and monitoring dysfunctional automatic thoughts; (b) creating an awareness of the connection between thoughts, emotions, and behaviors; and (c) evaluating the reasonableness of automatic thoughts and substituting more adaptive thoughts. Behavioral techniques may involve (a) monitoring and scheduling activities, (b) graded assignments, (c) behavioral rehearsal, and (d) relaxation and attention-refocusing methods.

The emphasis throughout cognitive-behavioral therapy is on skill building. Patients are instructed to practice new cognitive and behavioral strategies through homework assignments between therapy sessions. In addition, patients have the opportunity to trouble-shoot problems in applying these skills during therapy sessions. In this way, patients' progress toward becoming "their own therapist" is encouraged, and this shift is facilitated more and more as therapy progresses.

Cognitive-behavioral approaches tend to stress maintenance of change more than other theoretical schools. A number of therapy approaches assume that deep personality changes take place during therapy that allow the client to remain well without further efforts to sustain recovery (Shiffman, 1992).

Many of the arguments for using psychotherapy, in addition to or instead of pharmacotherapy, in the treatment of emotional disorders can also be used to support the role of psychotherapy in preventing relapse in these disorders. In the case of depression, for example, it has been found that although antidepressant medication is very effective in the acute treatment of depression, there is a high relapse rate. Weissman et al. (1974) have demonstrated that pharmacotherapy, without some form of structured psychotherapy, has a limited impact, especially in the long term, because symptom reduction does not necessarily bring with it social and interpersonal readjustment. Furthermore, although psychological factors are not addressed in chemotherapy, they are an important focus of structured psychotherapies, especially interpersonal psychotherapy (Klerman et al., 1984) and cognitive therapy (A. T. Beck et al., 1979). Also, patients receiving chemotherapy may well attribute change to the medication rather than to their own efforts and, as a consequence, may see relapses or setbacks as beyond their control.

It is clear that emotional disorders are multifaceted and complex, and they involve a reciprocal interaction between cognition, behavior, biochemical events, and affect, as well as current and previous stressors. Thus, simultaneous or sequential interventions that address these many different psychological, biological, and environmental influences may be required. Any treatment plan that helps patients to modify dysfunctional attitudes, problematic behavioral patterns, and troublesome life situations, while also correcting any chemical imbalance, would seem most likely to prevent relapse.

More specifically, A. T. Beck (1976) predicts that because dysfunctional attitudes may predispose to depression and these attitudes are modified in cognitive therapy, then cognitive therapy patients will be inoculated to some extent against relapse. Similarly, Blackburn, Eunson, and Bishop (1986) make the point that cognitive-behavioral therapy is a sophisticated treatment that deals not only with negatively biased thought content but also with negative attitudes and information-processing deficits that are considered to be depressogenic. Therefore, it could be predicted logically that patients who undergo cognitive therapy will learn new skills that they can then apply in the future if disturbances of mood reoccur. From a theoretical standpoint, one would expect that the ability to correct thoughts and attitudes that exacerbate or maintain depression and anxiety would have an inoculating effect without the need for further therapy. To what extent this prediction has been born out will be examined later.

Although most texts in the cognitive-behavioral area emphasize the importance of a maintenance and relapse-prevention focus, particularly in the later stages of therapy, there is no systematic body of work in the area of cognitive-behavioral treatment of Emotional Disorders comparable to that which now exists in the area of addictive behaviors (Chiauzzi, 1992; Marlatt & Gordon, 1985). The necessity for more practical guidelines on how to prevent relapse seems all the more important when one considers the research demonstrating that different factors are often involved in the relapse process than in the initial episode of depression (Lewinsohn, Sullivan, & Grossup, 1982). Therapy aimed at relapse-prevention will need to take this into account.

In general, it might be argued that acute treatment may be very different from relapse-prevention work (Shiffman, 1992). It behooves clinicians not to assume that a standard course of cognitive-behavioral treatment automatically inoculates the client against relapse.

DEFINITIONS OF RELAPSE

As Brownell et al. (1986) have pointed out, there are two very different dictionary definitions of the word relapse, each reflecting a bias concerning its nature and severity. The first is "a recurrence of symptoms of a disease after a period of improvement" (Brownell et al., 1986, p. 765). This refers to a specific outcome and implies dichotomous categories of well versus ill. The second definition is "the act or instance of backsliding, worsening or subsiding" (Brownell et al., 1986, p. 786). This refers to a process rather than an outcome and implies that something less serious (i.e., a slip, mistake, or regression) has occurred which may or may not lead to a full relapse. Whether the process or outcome definition of relapse is chosen has obvious implications for the conceptualization, prevention, and treatment of relapse. Viewing relapse as a process and not as an outcome implies that there are choice points in the process where the therapist and client can intervene. Therefore, the initial stage may involve a lapse which might mean the reemergence of a previous habit or set of symptoms. This stage may or may not lead to a full relapse. Whether this occurs is related to the degree to which corrective action is taken and how successful this action is. Put simply, the patient's response to the initial lapse will determine whether relapse will occur.

The definition of relapse as a process is consistent with the theoretical underpinnings of cognitive-behavioral approaches, while the definition of relapse as a recurrence of a disease is more consistent with a medical model of emotional disorder. This framework helps to maximize treatment gains by focusing on the acquisition of self-management skills so that relapse can be prevented or at least attenuated.

THE NEED FOR A GREATER EMPHASIS ON MAINTENANCE AND RELAPSE-PREVENTION IN PSYCHOTHERAPY

Although cognitive-behavioral approaches appear to have reduced the relapse rates in some emotional disorders, especially depression and panic/agoraphobia, a significant percentage of patients (approximately 20% to 35%) still experience a recurrence of symptoms (Ludgate, 1994). Despite the evidence that cognitive-behavioral therapy reduces the risk of relapse in controlled studies, this may be an even more significant problem for clinicians because it is usually the case that patients treated in clinical practice will have more severe psychopathology than patients meeting the inclusionary criteria for research studies.

There has been a great deal of emphasis on relapse-prevention in the clinical literature on addictions and eating disorders (Marlatt & Gordon, 1985; Mines & Merrill, 1987). A number of writers in the field of depression have recently described how maintenance and relapse-prevention can be built into a comprehensive treatment of depression (Frank et al., 1991; Miller, 1984). These and other writers have emphasized the distinctive features of maintenance treatment, including the need for increased client responsibility in the maintenance phase (Shiffman, 1992).

Knowledge of predictors of relapse or sustained recovery can guide good clinical practice in terms of relapse-prevention. For example, studies done on dysfunctional attitudes and relapse (Eaves & Rush, 1984; Ludgate, Reinecke, & A. T. Beck, 1987) suggest that unless patients' maladaptive attitudes or beliefs are identified and modified in therapy, patients who have improved symptomatically may still be at risk for relapse after treatment. It may be that psychotherapy which produces symptom-relief only is less than adequate treatment in terms of long-term outcome.

Although no studies have addressed this issue empirically, it seems likely that inadequate conceptualization and the application of cognitive-behavioral therapy in a rigid, overtechnical manner is associated with a higher risk of relapse because core and idiosyncratic problems are not identified and addressed. Consequently, there is a need for a comprehensive case assessment based on a biopsychosocial risk analysis to ensure well-planned and appropriate treatment. The importance of sophisticated case conceptualization as a means of maximizing treatment gains and preventing relapse needs to be underscored (Ludgate, 1994).

Finally, the focus on a skills-training approach with the patient being helped to become his or her "own therapist" would appear to be important in guiding clinical practice. This emphasis is consistent with self-efficacy research (Bandura, 1977) and with process research in cognitive therapy (Barber & DeRubeis, 1989). This research suggests that compensatory skills (i.e., skills to curtail negative thinking) are the process by which patients both overcome problems and prevent relapse. Also, in keeping with this model, Ludgate (1991) found that patients' perception of their skill in using cognitive therapy strategies on their own after therapy was the most powerful predictor of positive outcome over a 5-year period.

FACTORS IN RELAPSE

The following factors may be important in the relapse process. These factors can be targeted for intervention in a comprehensive treatment approach.

- the patient's personal resources and skills and his or her perception of these
- external resources including support systems such as family, friends, community, and professional help, and the perception of these resources
- life events/stressors and the patient's perceptions of these events
- biochemical events
- residual symptomatology at the end of treatment
- residual or continuing cognitive deficits or distortions such as dysfunctional beliefs or biased information processing after treatment

RELAPSE RATES IN EMOTIONAL DISORDERS

It is important before reviewing this area to distinguish between relapse and recurrence. Klerman (1978) defines relapse as a return of symptoms within 6 to 9 months of the onset of the index episode, while recurrence is defined as a return of symptoms after this period. In this section, studies on both recurrence of symptoms and relapse will be reported. In some cases, return to treatment is the criterion for relapse or recurrence. Studies in this area are often difficult to interpret and compare owing to the use of different definitions of relapse, recovery, and recurrence. There are also many other methodological difficulties in this area. Nonetheless, an attempt will be made to synthesize the findings in this area in order to give some idea of relapse rates for affective and anxiety disorders.

Depression. Of patients treated for depression, 70% to 95% will recover, but some 47% to 79% will have one or more recurrences, the correct figure probably being closer to 79% when longer follow-up periods are involved (A. T. Beck, 1967). With recurrent depressive episodes, the duration of episodes remains about the same, but the symptom-free intervals tend to decrease with each successive episode. Belsher and Costello (1988) in their review of relapse in depression concluded that "within 2 years of recovery around 50% of patients relapse" (p. 94). They also found that 20% of recovered patients will relapse within 2 months and 40% within 1 year.

Rates of relapse for patients using medication, either as treatment in the acute phase or as maintenance treatment, have been found to be in the 46% to 78% range. When compared to pharmacological methods, cognitive-behavioral treatments appear to reduce the risk of relapse, as can be seen in Table 1 (p. 10).

In reviewing the studies in Table 1 (p. 10), it is worth noting that relapse rates for patients treated with medication alone varied from 65% to 78%. In the one study where maintenance medication was used, the relapse rate was reduced to 50% over 2 years (Evans et al., 1985).

The outcome research in cognitive-behavioral therapy of depression, as shown in Table 1 (p. 10), suggests that cognitive-behavioral therapy has a significant prophylactic effect. Compared to those treated with pharmacotherapy alone, depressed outpatients who have undergone 12 to 20 sessions of cognitive-behavioral therapy appear to have roughly half the likelihood of relapsing over follow-up periods ranging from 1 to 2 years. Relapse rates for cognitive-behavioral therapy range from 22% to 38% while those for pharmacotherapy range from 65% to 78%.

In a 1-year outcome study, Kovacs et al. (1981) followed a sample of depressed patients who had responded to cognitive therapy (CT) or Imipramine at the end of treatment. They found that 39% of the CBT group and 65% of the Imipramine group had relapsed based upon a criterion score on a depression measure, while 50% of the cognitive therapy group and 75% of the Imipramine group had re-entered treatment.

In another 1-year follow-up study of depressed patients using similar criteria for relapse, Simons et al. (1986) found relapse rates of 20% for cognitive therapy, 66% for antidepressant treatment, and 43% for a combination of both. Using a somewhat more stringent criterion of relapse, Blackburn et al. (1986) found that only 23% of patients treated with cognitive-behavior therapy had relapsed over a 2-year period compared with 78% of patients treated with medication. In addition, relapse rates at 6 months, 1 year, and 18 months were significantly less for the cognitive-

TABLE 1: RELAPSE RATES FOR COGNITIVE-BEHAVIORAL THERAPY (CBT) AND PHARMACOLOGICAL TREATMENT (MED)

FOLLOW-UP PERIOD	STUDY	CBT	MED
1 year	Kovacs et al. (1981)	39%	65%
	Simons et al. (1986)	20%	66%
2 years	Blackburn et al. (1986)	23%	78%
	Evans et al. (1985)	30%	70% *50%
3 years	Gonzales et al. (1985)	36%	

Note: In interpreting this table, it should be realized that the criteria for relapse differ across studies.

* = Maintenance medication

behavior therapy group. Evans et al. (1985) found that only 30% of cognitive therapy patients relapsed over a 2-year follow-up period compared to 70% who were treated with medication during treatment and 50% who were maintained on medication following treatment.

Gonzales, Lewinsohn, and Clark (1985) followed up a large number of depressed outpatients who had received cognitive-behavior therapy for 1 to 3 years. Approximately half of the patients in this sample remained symptom-free throughout the 3-year follow-up period with 30% relapsing in the first year and 36% over the 3-year period.

In the only study which followed a clinical sample of depressed patients treated with cognitive therapy for 5 years, Ludgate (1991) found that (a) 32% had a recurrence of symptoms as severe as the index episode, while 39.7% had milder symptoms and

17.95% were symptom-free, (b) 52.1% met diagnostic criteria for an Affective Disorder during the 5-year period, and (c) 47.9% re-entered therapy, while 22% received psychotropic medication for depression.

Hollon and Najavits (1988), following a comprehensive review of studies on cognitive therapy and depression, concluded that there is strong convergent evidence that cognitive therapy provides greater protection against post-treatment relapse/recurrence than does tricyclic medication. Relapse rates tend to be in excess of 60% for pharmacotherapy versus 30% for cognitive therapy.

Although research suggests that cognitive-behavioral approaches offer some advantage in terms of prolonged recovery, it is worth noting that up to 40% of patients relapse over a 2-year period following cognitive-behavioral treatment (Ludgate, 1994). In clinical practice, most therapists are likely to observe that a significant number of patients treated successfully for depression will not sustain their recovery and will seek additional treatment. Despite lower relapse rates compared to other treatment modalities, relapse is still a significant problem in cognitive-behavior therapy. As a consequence, it behooves clinicians to refine and evaluate relapse-prevention methods to counter this.

Anxiety. There are few studies that follow patients with Generalized Anxiety Disorder (GAD) for any significant period of time post-treatment. In a review of the research on GAD, Rapee (1991) concluded that the positive treatment effects of psychotherapy tend to endure over 6- to 12-month follow-up periods. In one of the few studies that followed patients for more than 1 year, Holcomb (1986) found that patients who received Stress Inoculation Training (Meichenbaum, 1977) for severe stress and/or anxiety disorders required fewer readmissions over a 3-year follow-up period than did a group of patients treated with medication.

Using Anxiety Management Training that incorporated cognitive-behavioral methods, Butler et al. (1987) found that, of the patients who responded to this treatment, 68% did not contact their family practitioners over a 1-year period following treatment. No studies of the longer term effects of medication alone exist to compare these results to.

However, in the area of agoraphobia, Telch, Tearnan, and Taylor (1983) found relapse rates of 27% to 50% in patients treated with antidepressants. The long-term effects of cognitive-behavioral treatment for agoraphobia seem somewhat equivocal. For example, Barlow and Wolfe (1981) show that 60% to 70% respond to exposure treatments in the short-term, but as few as 18% remain symptom free at follow-up. Although they define relapse rather broadly as "any reduction in treatment gains," Munby and Johnston (1980) reported that 50% of those who show a clinical response relapsed over a 1-year period. Emmelkamp and Kuipers (1979) report that 60% to 70% of their agoraphobic patients treated with cognitive-behavioral therapy maintain their improvement at a 4-year follow-up and other researchers have reported similar positive long-term effects.

In the treatment of panic disorder, medication is often very effective at eliminating panic attacks in the short-term. However, Fyer et al. (1987) have found up to a 90% relapse rate following discontinuation of Alprazolam, one of the most frequently used of these medications. In contrast, Zitrin, Klein, and Woerner (1980) found a relapse rate of 29% over 4 to 10 years when psycho-therapy methods such as exposure are used in combination with Imipramine. In their review of the treatment of Panic Disorder with Agoraphobia, Michelson and Marchione (1991) found that cognitive-behavior therapy produced lower relapse rates than medication. Furthermore, when cognitive-behavioral therapy was administered in combination with medication, it decreased the relapse rate compared with medication alone. Salkovskis, Jones, and Clark (1986) found an almost total elimination of panic attacks during a 2-year follow-up period in panic disorder patients treated with cognitive therapy.

A great number of psychotherapy outcome studies have been carried out in the area of Obsessive-Compulsive Disorder, especially those using behavioral and cognitive-behavioral methods. In reviewing these studies, Foa et al. (1983) reported relapse rates for patients successfully treated with these methods of 20% to 25% in follow-up periods ranging from 4 months to 3 years. In a 5- to 6-year follow-up study of Obsessive-Compulsive Disorder patients, Meyer, Levy, and Schnurer (1974) found that only 17% had relapsed.

Despite a growing literature on psychotherapy with other anxiety disorders, such as Post-Traumatic Stress Disorder, Simple Phobia, and Social Phobia, no methodologically adequate long-term follow-up studies are reported in the literature. In summary, follow-up studies of relapse rates for patients with anxiety disorders are somewhat equivocal, but do suggest that patients treated with cognitive-behavior therapy have a lower risk of relapse. Again, as in the field of depression, it is clear that a significant proportion of patients will not maintain treatment gains and will experience a recurrence of symptoms. Clinicians and clinical researchers need to develop more effective methods of relapse-prevention to help these patients.

PREDICTORS OF RELAPSE

In this section, particular emphasis will be placed on predictors of sustained recovery or relapse which have obvious implications for clinical practice and can help to inform and direct psychotherapy with emotionally distressed clients.

Depression. In a review of outcome studies in the treatment of depression, Belsher and Costello (1988) found that the influence of life stress on relapse is now well established. The presence of recurrent episodes of depression also seems to be associated with poorer outcome. Furthermore, they concluded that demographic variables, with the exception of age, have not been demonstrated conclusively to be associated with relapse or sustained recovery. The role of social support in producing positive outcome also appears to be empirically demonstrated. Belsher and Costello contend that risk factors for relapse in depression are (a) high levels of environmental stress, (b) the absence of social support from family members, (c) a history of recurrent depressive episodes, and (d) persistent neuroendocrine dysregulation after recovery from a depressive episode. Although some of these factors are fixed and therefore not amenable to therapeutic efforts (age, previous history), there are obvious therapeutic implications for relapse-prevention in some of the other findings. Specifically, attempts to provide patients with methods to deal with future environmental stress, increasing social support, and, for those patients with biological dysregulation, continuing pharmacological interventions after the acute depressive episode should help to reduce the risk of depressive relapse.

Other variables that have emerged as predictors of relapse in the psychotherapeutic treatment of depression (Evans et al., 1985; Gonzales et al., 1985; Kovacs et al., 1981; Ludgate, 1991; Simons et al., 1986) are reported in Table 2 (below).

On the issue of personality disorders as a predictor of poor outcome, it should be noted that Thompson, Gallagher, and Czirr (1988) found that cognitive-behavioral treatment of depression in an elderly population was less effective when a concomitant personality disorder existed. In contrast, other studies (Ludgate, 1991; Persons, Burns, & Parloff, 1988) have found that the presence of a personality disorder does not influence the outcome in cognitive-behavioral treatment of depression. Also, it is worth

---

TABLE 2: PREDICTORS OF POOR LONG-TERM OUTCOME IN THE PSYCHOTHERAPY OF DEPRESSION

---

1. Negative patient characteristics

    • Presence of an Axis II disorder
    • Less pre-treatment resourcefulness
    • Patients' lowered perception of their ability to apply cognitive therapy skills after treatment

2. End of treatment variables

    • Higher levels of residual depression
    • Higher levels of hopelessness
    • Higher levels of dysfunctional attitudes
    • Global and external attributional style

3. External factors

    • More environmental stress/life events
    • Less satisfaction with life roles
    • Less social support

---

noting that Ludgate (1991) found that the 5-year outcome did not differ for dysthymic and major depression patients. This may be encouraging to clinicians and prevent them from prematurely labeling patients with a concurrent Axis II disorder and an Affective Disorder as having a poor prognosis. It is also important to note that age, severity, duration, and history were not predictive of relapse in this study. The only significant predictors of relapse were (a) patients' perception of their skill in being able to apply cognitive therapy methods to their problems at follow-up, and (b) total number of stressful life events during the follow-up period. In addition, higher levels of depression at end of treatment appear to be a weak predictor of long-term outcome.

The implications of these findings in terms of maintenance and relapse-prevention are

- Before termination, therapy should focus on correcting those cognitive distortions (including dysfunctional attitudes and attributional style) that predispose to relapse after therapy.
- Residual depressive symptoms and hopelessness should be addressed before therapy is terminated.
- Where an Axis II personality disorder exists, therapy should focus on issues related to the personality disorder as well as the depression.
- General problem-solving skills should be taught and practiced regularly.
- Self-efficacy and perception of ability to use self-control methods should be fostered.
- Future life stressors should be anticipated and planned for, where possible.
- Significant others should be involved in treatment, if possible, and support systems set up before therapy ends.
- Therapy should focus on life roles and lifestyle and promote changes in these areas, where necessary.

Lastly, following from Ludgate's (1991) finding that stressful life events, in conjunction with patients' perceptions that they possess adequate cognitive therapy skills, are the most potent predictors of sustained recovery/relapse, it is probable that patients will do better over the long-term if they either have fewer stressful life events (a variable which cannot be controlled) or if they perceive themselves to be in possession of coping skills that will help them to deal with the challenges produced by stressful life events.

This would involve training patients in "meta cognitive skills," that is, the ability to reflect on one's own thinking, to evaluate the accuracy of specific thoughts, and to generate alternatives that can be logically or empirically tested. The learning of specific coping responses is likely to give patients a sense of control over their depression. This may, in turn, help to prevent the "depression about depression" that often occurs when patients experience some mild recurrence of symptoms after treatment (Teasdale, 1985).

Anxiety. It has been found that patients' characteristics also influence the long-term outcome in the treatment of anxiety disorders. Turner (1987) has shown that the cognitive-behavioral treatment of social anxiety is not as effective when a concomitant personality disorder exists. Also, negative life events have been implicated in the long-term outcome of patients treated for anxiety disorders (Munroe & Wade, 1988). Factors in the interpersonal domain (rejection, loss, marital conflict) and physical/health area (childbirth, surgery, loss of health) have also been cited by some authors as important in the course of anxiety disorders (Tearnan, Telch, & Keefe, 1984). An association between life stress and outcome has consistently been found in the treatment of agoraphobia.

Brown and Harris (1978) suggest that individuals experiencing threat rather than loss are more likely to be both anxious and depressed rather than depressed alone. The effects of stressful life events on anxiety disorders and the effect on treatment response or maintenance of gains has not been extensively researched. Unfortunately, many studies in this area have combined initial onset and relapse groups, thus making interpretation of results difficult.

Rapee (1991) has hypothesized that information-processing deficits are implicated in the maintenance of anxiety disorders. In this regard, Generalized Anxiety Disorder patients are hypothesized to be more likely to associate various stimulus information with threat, and cites evidence to support this hypothesis in experimental studies. In addition, threat sensitive patients also have been found to have a perception of uncontrollability over threatening events. According to the cognitive model, the interaction of these two factors may predispose individuals to experience clinically significant levels of anxiety. As a consequence, psychotherapy that aims to prevent relapse should focus on identifying and correcting faulty beliefs regarding the presence of threat and "uncontrollability."

OVERVIEW OF STRATEGIES FOR
MAINTENANCE AND RELAPSE-PREVENTION

Although many writers in the cognitive-behavior therapy field stress the importance of building maintenance and relapse-prevention into treatment, little information exists as to how this can be achieved in actual practice or which techniques are most useful in this endeavor.

Krantz et al. (1984) carried out a survey of cognitive-behavioral researchers and clinicians, asking them to rate their use of different strategies to promote maintenance. Greenwald (1988) has made a number of suggestions concerning strategies for promoting maintenance in Anxiety Disorders. From these and other clinical sources, the following appear to be the most promising therapy strategies for practitioners:

- fade frequency of sessions later in therapy
- use booster/refresher sessions
- increase patient responsibility within sessions
- place greater emphasis on between-session activities/homework as therapy proceeds
- get the patient to practice beyond criterion and overlearn
- promote internal attributions of change

- work on a variety of targets
- train in general skills and *in vivo*, where appropriate
- enlist significant others in therapy
- educate regarding relapse and create realistic expectations regarding the future course of the disorder
- discuss the need for and the benefits of maintenance efforts
- help the patient to develop a self-therapy program to be used after termination
- identify barriers to change or problems stemming from changes
- anticipate and plan for high-risk situations
- involve the patient in generating an emergency plan in the event of future setbacks
- modify the environment, where possible, to support new behaviors or responses

The preceding procedures emphasize the need for (a) collaboration, (b) training in general skills and strategies, (c) the development of problem-solving skills, and (d) anticipating and planning for setbacks. Selecting specific strategies to aid a particular client in maintaining treatment gains and preventing relapse will obviously require both flexibility and individual consideration based on a detailed case conceptualization. A. T. Beck et al. (1979) suggest that behavioral strategies may be most important in producing initial change while cognitive techniques may be more important in the maintenance or consolidation phase. Generally, the combination of both will hold the most promise in terms of both initial and long-term positive outcome.

SPECIFIC PROCEDURES FOR
MAINTENANCE AND RELAPSE-PREVENTION

A number of procedures and strategies that are applicable to both emotionally distressed outpatients and inpatients and that can be utilized in individual or group Cognitive-Behavioral Therapy will be described here as they pertain to the different phases of therapy.

EARLY THERAPY ACTIVITIES

Assessment of Relapse Risk. During the assessment phase and also in the early stages of treatment when data is being gathered, the therapist should carry out a comprehensive individual case conceptualization and identify risk factors for relapse for each patient. Treatment strategies can then be devised with these in mind. Matching treatment to the pertinent issues and under-pinnings of the patient's depression or anxiety can then be achieved. This may be one of the most important aspects of relapse-prevention and helps provide a broad based, compre-hensive, and patient-centered therapy focus.

For example, Jenny,* a patient who presented with a recurrent severe depression, was conceptualized as having a deep-seated belief regarding her own inadequacy and a corresponding need for "a man in my life to depend on." These depressogenic beliefs appeared to become activated by relationship problems with her husband. Consequently, they were targeted as an area for thera-peutic intervention in an effort to both combat her depression and to reduce the risk of subsequent relapse.

Graph of Progress. It may be important in the first therapy session to discuss with the patient his or her expectations concern-ing both the time frame of therapy and the likely course of thera-peutic progress. Where expectations are unrealistic, for example the patient with an Axis II disorder expects to be "cured" within six or seven sessions, these can be adjusted. Also the therapist can demonstrate by means of graphs the manner in which progress may occur and the reasons for this. The graph will show a gen-eral trend towards improvement, but with some weekly/daily fluctuations. This will help prevent the patient from catastro-phizing if progress is not maintained in a linear and cumulative way.

---

*Names and identifying characteristics of persons in all case examples have been disguised thoroughly to protect privacy.

Anticipating Termination and Stressing the Therapist's Goal of Making Patients Function as Their Own Therapist. Early in therapy, the therapist should stress that termination will not be time-based, but progress-based. Throughout therapy, termination should be discussed with the patient and preparation carried out for eventual termination. This preparation ideally would start in the first session. The therapist should stress the importance of maintenance and relapse-prevention at the earliest opportunity, and the patient should be given the expectation that therapy will provide him or her with self-control methods that can be used without the therapist after termination.

Emphasizing the Self-Help, Collaborative Focus of Therapy. Related to the above is the importance of stressing the openness, collaborative empiricism, and team approach of cognitive-behavioral therapy. The patient in the initial treatment phase should be provided with a good rationale for active involvement in therapy that includes giving feedback to the therapist, influencing session agendas, designing and completing homework assignments, and setting targets for therapy. The concept of collaboration needs to be carefully explained to the patient, and the advantages of this team approach should be repeatedly stressed.

The above-referenced explanations will facilitate the shift later in therapy towards the patient working on maintenance and relapse-prevention on his or her own.

THROUGHOUT THERAPY ACTIVITIES

Regular Patient Review of Skills. It is important that the patient understand and be able to verbalize the steps involved in the therapy process. He or she should be encouraged to review these regularly both within therapy sessions and as a homework assignment. The patient can be asked the following questions to facilitate this:

- What tools or skills do you have at this point to deal with your problems?

- What have you learned in therapy so far?
- What is different now from before, and what are you doing to make this happen?

As therapy proceeds, it will be useful to ask patients at regular intervals (e.g., every three or four sessions) to review and then write down what they have learned in therapy and what skills they now possess. This has the effect of helping patients recall skills learned and emphasizes at each point the range of behaviors or strategies available to them.

Patients should also be asked to review their goals and the principles of cognitive-behavioral therapy regularly as this will tend to keep patients active in the therapy process and also reinforce learning.

Patient Self-Monitoring of Progress. Patients can also be encouraged to regularly use self-rating scales, such as the Beck Depression Inventory (A. T. Beck et al., 1961), the State-Trait Anxiety Inventory (Speilberger, 1983), or the Beck Anxiety Inventory (A. T. Beck et al., 1988), while in treatment. As therapy proceeds, the patient can take more and more responsibility for completing, scoring, and interpreting these. Graphing or scaling progress in a visual way (see Appendix A, p. 61) may prove helpful for some clients and reinforce progress. The therapist should also give the patient feedback regarding progress, as well as which skills are working. The patient's sense of self-efficacy is likely to be enhanced by these activities.

Overpractice of Skills (Overlearning). Research and clinical practice strongly suggest that maintaining progress and change is facilitated by getting patients to practice newly acquired cognitive and behavioral skills beyond "competence" levels. This overlearning will ensure that these coping skills become an automatic part of the patient's repertoire and will increase the chances of such skills being utilized after treatment ends. It would appear to be particularly important for the therapist and patient to collaboratively assess the durability of certain key skills during the later phases of therapy. The advantages of regular practice and the benefits of making these skills reflexive or habitual should be repeatedly stressed.

Teaching Skills With Wide Application. This involves what is described as a "meta cognitive orientation," in which methods of problem solving or thought-testing can be readily applied to a variety of current problem situations, as well as to future problems. This is consistent with the concept of providing the patient with generic self-therapy methods. The patient should not only be provided with tools to deal with specific upsetting situations but should be taught general problem-solving skills using role reversal, modeling, imagery, and other methods to foster learning. Skill-training should be initiated across many situations and involve multiple trials and tasks. This often works particularly well in a hospital situation where the staff are able to work in an integrated way. For example, Bill, a patient who was treated in an inpatient cognitive therapy program, had his perfectionism and all-or-nothing thinking challenged and modified throughout his hospital stay in group cognitive therapy, in activity therapy tasks, and by nursing staff on the unit.

Generalizing Skills/Tools. Related to the preceding is the need to focus on efforts to foster generalization of skills. A good rationale needs to be given for this and the importance of generalization should be stressed to the patient throughout. Every opportunity to transfer skills used in one situation to other situations should be exploited fully by the therapist. A discussion on common principles and intervention procedures that generalize across problem situations should be initiated after each situation-specific intervention has been executed.

Modeling, coaching, feedback, and homework assignments are important, as well as instructing the patient in self-reinforcement strategies.

Some common tools that patients undergoing cognitive-behavioral treatment may be expected to have in their repertoire for use both during and after therapy might include

- Identifying and testing negative thoughts.
- Recognizing distorted thinking patterns.
- Rationally responding to automatic thoughts.
- Identifying and revising underlying beliefs.
- Generating alternative behavioral or cognitive response options.
- Cost-benefit analysis of beliefs/choices.
- Affect and arousal-reduction methods, for example, relaxation, distraction, breathing control.
- Activity monitoring and scheduling.
- Creating hierarchies of difficult tasks.

Forms that are useful in prompting patients to use these skills on their own are included in Appendices B and C (pp. 63-66).

Working at the Schema/Belief Level. Toward the later stages of therapy, after symptom-relief has occurred, the therapist will need to work on beliefs or schemas that increase the likelihood of relapse for certain patients. This will be especially important in patients diagnosed with an Axis II disorder, but will also be necessary with depressed or anxious patients who have dysfunctional beliefs such as "I must be perfect," "I have to be in control," or "I am weak and a victim." In addition, investigating and uncovering beliefs about therapeutic progress and self-efficacy may be critical in facilitating a self-therapy focus once actual therapy is completed.

Dealing With Axis II Issues Where Necessary. As shown earlier, some studies have shown that the presence of an Axis II personality disorder makes cognitive-behavioral treatment less effective in anxious and depressed clients. Therefore, efforts to use cognitive-behavioral methods to deal with issues related to Axis II personality disorders (A. T. Beck & Freeman, 1990; Young, 1994) in the later stages of therapy are likely to prove beneficial in terms of relapse-prevention.

Making the Patient More Active in Therapy. Ideally, as therapy proceeds, the patient's perception of his or her role in the therapy process should be more and more as a trainee. This will entail a problem-solving, collaborative focus rather than a view of himself or herself as a sick person with the implication that only external help will be effective. The patient's sense of responsibility and control should be increased as therapy proceeds and he or she becomes more involved in agenda setting and homework. The therapist, conversely, will become less active and will adopt more of a consultative rather than a directive role as therapy proceeds.

Explanation for Progress/Attributions Regarding Change. The therapist needs to ask probing questions in an effort to promote internal rather than external attributions for improvement and external rather than internal attributions for lapses or setbacks. In some cases, this will involve exposing a double standard in patients' thinking, such as "I got better because of life changes" and "I slipped back because I'm weak." Meichenbaum (1977) argues that it is essential that patients acknowledge that meaningful changes have been made and attribute these changes to their own efforts rather than to the therapist or to environmental factors for true maintenance to take place.

It is important to get patients to review not just what has changed or what behavioral or cognitive competencies or coping skills have been acquired, but also what meanings are attributed to such changes. It may be necessary for the therapist to use guided discovery to facilitate the development in the patient of a more appropriate and helpful attributional style. Identifying and correcting any distortions in thinking that result in external, specific attributions for progress and internal, global attributions for relapses are especially important in this regard.

The therapist should attempt to link improvement to the patient's competence and/or efforts and, in this way, strengthen beliefs about self-efficacy.

Predicting Automatic Thoughts About a Setback. Prior to the time when the patient may begin to experience a setback within the active therapy period, it can be very useful to ask the patient to imagine experiencing a setback and to predict what he or she will be thinking at this point. Based on previous experience, patients may predict thoughts like "I shouldn't be feeling this way," "I'm hopeless, I'll never get well," "It's not fair," or "This therapy isn't working." Such anticipated self-statements give clues to the patient's belief system and can be combated in advance of any real setbacks. It can also be helpful to get the patient to identify the cognitive distortions, for example, mind-reading, all-or-nothing thinking, overgeneralization, and filtering, present in such thinking (A. T. Beck, 1976).

Responding to Negative Thoughts About a Setback. Either in the previously mentioned imagined scenario or in the event of a naturally occurring slipback during therapy, the therapist should exploit this situation by helping the patient to respond cognitively to this event in a more functional way. The same methods of testing and answering negative automatic thoughts that are a critical part of cognitive-behavior therapy can be utilized here. For example, a patient who feels discouraged and helpless in the face of a recurrence of symptoms may be helped to identify his or her negative thoughts about this event, such as "I am back to square one" or "This means therapy is not working." He or she can then begin to test these thoughts by asking himself or herself, "What is the evidence for this thought," "What is another way of looking at this situation," "What is the worst/most realistic outcome," "What can I do," and so forth (see Appendix B, pp. 63-64).

Involving Significant Others in Treatment. In many cases relatives may inadvertently reinforce symptoms of depression and anxiety, and this will tend to maintain or precipitate recurrence of these problems if the family are not involved. Couple and family interventions using a cognitive-behavioral model (Dattilio & Padesky, 1990; Epstein, Schlessinger, & Dryden, 1988) can be used where necessary. Less formally, attempts to maximize treatment gains and prevent relapse via the involvement of significant others might involve (a) educating the family regarding the nature, course, and treatment of the disorder; (b) outlining the rationale, goals, and strategies of cognitive-behavioral therapy; (c) educating family members about early warning signs; and (d) outlining the strategies and helpful responses the family can use in the recovery or relapse stages. Self-help books, such as *Feeling Good* (Burns, 1981) and *Coping With Panic* (Clum, 1990) may be of considerable assistance in facilitating an understanding of and more appropriate responses to patients' problem behaviors in relatives of patients experiencing depression or anxiety.

Increasing Emphasis on Between Session Behavior. Although cognitive-behavioral approaches characteristically stress homework and between-session patient activity, this focus should become even more pronounced as therapy proceeds so that the emphasis is shifted more and more from solving problems within the therapy sessions to supervising the patients' application of cognitive methods to their problems outside sessions. In this way, patients take greater control and responsibility for helping themselves. Also, in addition to monitoring their own symptoms, as described earlier (see Appendix A, p. 61), patients' activity levels in therapy can be increased by keeping daily records of dysfunctional thoughts or panic logs throughout therapy. Regular practice in self-monitoring and recording at this point will ensure that it becomes more automatic after termination when the patient will need to continue self-maintenance efforts.

Self-monitoring will also help to offset biased observation and information retrieval. A behavioral record that includes thoughts, feelings, and actions also serves an important function as a stable archive for hypothesis-testing (Greenwald, 1988).

NEAR TERMINATION ACTIVITIES

Gradual Tapering/Spacing of Sessions. As termination approaches, most cognitive-behavior therapists incorporate fading of therapy sessions in a systematic way while also being sensitive to changing patient needs. This should be done collaboratively with the patient and reviewed regularly. Most importantly, the rationale for this, that is, increasing the patient's responsibility and ability to be his or her own therapist, should be stressed. This can be viewed and presented to the patient as a dress rehearsal for eventual termination and as a no-fail experiment to evaluate the patient's self-reliance or progress.

Exploring Thoughts Regarding Termination. It is important, as mentioned earlier, that termination issues be dealt with from the beginning of therapy. In the closing phase of therapy, the therapist should make sure to elicit from the client cognitions about the upcoming termination by asking questions, such as "What are your feelings and thoughts about leaving therapy or not seeing me regularly?" In a more general way, the therapist can also ask, "How does the immediate future, that is, after therapy, look to you?" Reported automatic negative thoughts, such as "I won't be able to handle my life on my own" or "I'll have no one to turn to if problems come up" can then be dealt with using cognitive interventions.

Overall Review of Skills and Progress. As part of a general review to facilitate a sense of self-efficacy, the patient can be asked at this point in therapy, "What have you achieved in therapy?" "What is different now and what specifically did you do to make this happen?" (This will prompt an internal attribution.) "What have you learned and what tools do you now have to deal with your problems?"

All of the preceding questions can be used both in session and as homework assignments to prevent negative filtering, as well as to correct or avoid a failure bias. This is particularly helpful with inpatients who have done very well in the hospital milieu but who are concerned that they will relapse when away from the supportive, less-stressful hospital environment. These patients should be encouraged to list both what they will leave behind on discharge (e.g., the staff, fellow patients, the structured program) and what they will take with them (e.g., specific strategies to control negative thinking, stress, or low self-esteem).

Orientation to Maintenance and Relapse-Prevention. It is important to promote and establish an appropriate cognitive set for future coping. Implicit in this task is the provision of education regarding relapse, exploring the meaning of lapses to the patient, eliciting any unrealistic expectations regarding the future, and also establishing the need for and the benefits of continued maintenance efforts.

Education Regarding Recovery and Relapse. This can also be done at the earlier stages of therapy but is especially important at the later stages of therapy. When appropriate, a discussion of the nature of the patient's disorder and its usual course can be initiated. Also, expectations regarding the patient's prognosis, in the light of previous history and other factors, can be discussed.

It is particularly crucial that depressed patients be made aware of the risk of relapse, while also being given a hopeful message that detection of early warning signs and prompt intervention can often avert a full relapse. It is incumbent upon the therapist to create realistic expectations about relapse and recovery. As noted previously, this is very important particularly in the areas of depression and anxiety given the risk of relapse in these disorders. In Axis II patients, setbacks are also very likely. It is probably countertherapeutic to not discuss the risk of relapse with such patients as this may serve to set the patient up for future disappointment.

Patients may be asked at this point, "What are your thoughts regarding the future?" "Are these realistic?" "Do they contain any distortions?" "What might be a more realistic or functional way to think?" Patients should be led to expect that recovery is a continuous process over time and is not an all-or-nothing or time-limited event. In addition, patients should be prepared for the fact that the process of recovery may be cumulative, that overall progress will be incremental but probably not linear over time. Every day should not necessarily be expected to be better than the day before in terms of symptomatic distress. Also, patients leaving inpatient or day-treatment settings, as well as any patient who has been involved in lengthy or intensive treatment, should be led to expect some mild relapse after discharge. A rationale should be given for this, as well as suggestions for how to cope with this setback. All of the preceding will encourage patients to see recovery from a longer term perspective rather than expecting to be "cured" at the end of active treatment. This perspective will make it more likely that patients will see the need to continue to work on their issues and use the maintenance methods outlined here. Issues concerning the unfairness of having to take responsibility for future gains may emerge and can be dealt with at this point.

The Meaning of Relapse. It is important to explore patients' cognitions regarding the recurrence of symptoms. Patients may perceive symptom recurrence in a number of different ways. The manner in which symptom recurrence is construed has a significant effect on a patient's mood and behavior. It is therefore important to encourage the patient to perceive symptom recurrence as a setback or lapse rather than as complete failure. Thoughts associated with the perception of failure include the following: "I'm hopeless; I'll never get well," "This means therapy has failed," or "I'm doomed to be depressed again." Any cognitive distortions associated with the perception of failure can be explored. These negative thoughts can then be challenged in the standard way that cognitive-behavioral therapy deals with dysfunctional cognitions.

As Brownell et al. (1986) pointed out, therapists can adopt an outcome definition of relapse that involves a recurrence of a disease process after a period of initial improvement or a process definition of relapse that has very different therapy implications and involves an instance of backsliding or worsening of symptoms. Therapists and patients would appear to be better served by a process definition of relapse. A number of cognitive variables are involved in the progression from lapse to relapse. Consequently, it is important for the therapist to look at the individual's cognitive and behavioral response to an initial lapse.

Marlatt and Gordon (1985) recommended getting the patient to view a lapse as a learning process. They recommended that the therapist promote the notion that a lapse can lead to a prolapse, that is, a move forward after a setback, provided that the patient uses this opportunity to make changes and keeps a cognitive set that involves a problem-solving approach. The cognitive set that the therapist will be attempting to induce in the patient involves the use of self-statements, such as, "I hate feeling these symptoms of depression again, but instead of panicking I will see what I can do and maybe, if I make a plan and follow through with it, I won't get all the way down again this time."

The therapist can help the patient rehearse such functional cognitions in advance. The patient can be encouraged to go back and analyze his or her reactions to previous lapses. Alternatively, the therapist can get the patient to use imagery to visualize a lapse, or the therapist can present case scenarios of other patients who have lapsed in individual or group sessions. All of these techniques can then be used to test the patient's ability to come up with effective cognitive and behavioral strategies to deal with a setback.

Recognizing Early Warning Signs. In order to short-circuit the relapse process, the therapist can encourage the patient to identify early warning signs or prodromal symptoms that lead to relapse. If the patient is unable to identify early warning signs or prodromal symptoms, the therapist may be able to educate the patient regarding this pattern from an analysis of previous recurrences. The advantages of early recognition and intervention are emphasized as a rationale for identifying early warning signs of relapse.

It is particularly important for discharged or terminated patients who are not in contact with mental health professionals to become familiar with their personal early warning signals and learn how they can monitor and respond to these. Unless they become adept at recognizing early warning signs, early intervention will not be possible. Patients can be asked, "What are possible early warning signs of a recurrence that you need to be alert to?" The patient may identify disturbed sleep, social withdrawal, and/or irritability as key early symptoms in the development of depression.

A system of regular monitoring of these and other symptoms can then be set up. This can be done by getting the patient to refer to a simple symptom checklist (see Appendix D, p. 67) or to complete a self-report scale, like the Beck Depression Inventory or the Beck Anxiety Inventory. The patient can score, interpret, and chart these scales in a notebook (see Appendix A, p. 61). A panic/anxiety episode log or dysfunctional thought record (A. T. Beck et al., 1979) could also be used to monitor early warning signs. The therapist will normally institute this type of self-monitoring at the end of treatment and then get the patient to continue this after discharge. The patient can complete these systematic self-assessments on a regular, for example, weekly or monthly basis as part of a maintenance plan (Krantz, 1987). This will help patients to monitor their progress on their own and thus increase self-efficacy. More importantly, patients will learn to become aware of subtle and specific changes in mood or thinking and to take action to combat lapses before the lapses become more severe and incapacitating.

Anticipating High-Risk Situations. The therapist in the later part of therapy should spend time helping the patient to recognize or identify high-risk situations in order to avoid setbacks. The patient can be asked, "What are possible high-risk situations for you?" "When are times that you might possibly slip back, if you are not careful?" "What situations might put you back into a depressed or anxious state?"

The therapist and patient may go over the patient's past experience to identify triggers or to examine the patient's specific vulnerabilities. For example, a depressed patient may identify the anniversary of a loved one's death as a "difficult time" for him or her in terms of depressed feelings, or an anxious patient may have a speaking engagement coming up which has been found to be anxiety-provoking in the past. Although not all future stressors can be anticipated and many life events will by nature be unexpected, the advantages of being prepared for predictable, problematic situations can be strongly emphasized. The rationale for this approach is "forewarned is forearmed."

The Social Readjustment Scale (Holmes & Rahe, 1967) can be used as another method of eliciting possible high-risk situations when a patient cannot spontaneously come up with them. In this approach, the patient is asked if any of the listed life events are likely to occur in the post-discharge period. Once some high-risk situations have been identified, the next step is to collaboratively develop an active plan in advance to deal with them.

Emergency Plan for Setbacks. In the later phase of therapy, efforts should be directed towards both planning and rehearsing an "emotional fire drill" (Lazurus & Fay, 1984) both in and between therapy sessions. Both cognitive and behavioral rehearsal are useful here. Patients can work on this in therapy in a number of ways. They can be asked the question, "What things will you do in the event of a setback or when you notice some early warning signs of slipping back?" They can be encouraged to write down either all options or specific relapse-prevention plans on paper. These can be looked at by the therapist and patient collaboratively to see whether each is likely to be an effective coping strategy and also to ascertain if there are any drawbacks or problems attached to any of these strategies; for example, the use of alcohol to cope with stress. The most effective of these coping strategies can then be selected, and the therapist can also suggest additional coping strategies.

Coping strategies can then be ordered in terms of the sequence in which they might best be used and the conditions under which they might best be utilized; for example, if using a dysfunctional thought record does not help, the patient should then call his or her therapist. These strategies can be written on cards, possibly in the form of a flow chart. These flash cards should be carried around or at least be readily available to prompt the individual experiencing a lapse into action. These strategies, if necessary, could also be recorded on tape. The flash card or tape, which should ideally be written or recorded by patients themselves, can be used as part of a regular review, as well as when needed in critical periods. An anxious patient at the end of treatment wrote on such a card, "When I'm anxious I can (a) do a Dysfunctional Thought Record, (b) distract myself (clean out my pocketbook, talk to my husband), (c) do relaxation and breathing exercises, (d) focus on the task at hand, (e) just stay with it and notice any signs of the anxiety coming down, (f) exercise, or (g) call my therapist" (J. S. Beck, 1994).

Additionally, the therapist can test the patient's emergency plan by playing devil's advocate or can role-play the patient's characteristic negative thoughts to prepare for future challenges. Marlatt and Gordon (1985) advocated the use of programmed re- lapse in the cognitive-behavioral treatment of addictions. With depressed or anxious patients, induction of depressed mood or panic/anxiety attacks could be set up in sessions near the end of therapy in order to test the patients' coping skills.

Alternatively, instructing patients deliberately not to respond to automatic negative thoughts, in order to allow depression to build up so that patients can then practice working on the depression, could be instituted. Also, the therapist could use spontaneous lapses that occur in the course of therapy as opportunities to develop resilience or "emotional hardiness." By such means, the patient's confidence that he or she can get back on track can be increased.

Encouraging Early Help-Seeking. As part of the previously referenced emergency plan, the patient can be encouraged to seek help, if necessary, as soon as possible. In some instances, the patient may first try a number of rehearsed strategies once he or she notices the early warning signs of a relapse. If these rehearsed strategies are not effective, professional contact may be re-instituted. It may be helpful to work out in advance with the patient a specific plan in this regard, as well as to set specific criteria for seeking help again, for example, the presence of particular symptoms of a certain severity that persist for a certain time period. It may be necessary to help the patient frame this as "taking care of myself" rather than as "I can't make it alone and need my therapist again." It is worth noting that the patient should avoid all-or-nothing thinking in facing the prospect of a setback or lapse, for example, "I must never call my therapist" or "At any sign of slipback, I must get hold of my therapist" and instead should come up with a specific plan for how to deal with setbacks and lapses.

Relapse Rehearsal. Late in therapy, the patient's problem-solving skills can be probed by asking a series of questions to encourage the patient to "think the unthinkable" and actively plan how he or she will cope in the event of a relapse. A range of possible relapse situations can be generated in the manner suggested previously for identifying high-risk situations, and these can be explored carefully for both implications (cognitive impact) and actions (behavioral and problem-solving capacities). As with any skill acquisition, relapse rehearsal often involves therapist modeling and coaching, as well as behavioral rehearsal and corrective feedback. Rehearsal via projected imagery or "emotional fire drills" is also a powerful way to orient patients towards future coping.

Billings and Moos (1982) have classified coping strategies into (a) appraisal-focused (attempts to define the meaning of situations), (b) problem-focused (attempts to modify or eliminate the source of the distress), and (c) emotion-focused (efforts to manage the emotions generated). Patients can be instructed in strategies from each of these categories and encouraged to practice these strategies in sessions and as homework assignments.

Planning Self-Therapy Program. In addition to the specific plans generated to deal with setbacks, patients should also be asked, "How can you continue to use the skills you have learned in therapy in your everyday life?" They should be encouraged to write down ways of practicing the skills they have learned and instructed to record a step-by-step self-therapy plan. For example, an anxious patient might come up with the following list of activities to be continued after therapy:

- Do breathing exercises once a day.
- Write down thoughts when I need to.
- Read over old therapy notes once a month.
- Do one thing I really enjoy every day.
- Break down tasks into small steps every day.
- Use problem-solving procedures whenever I encounter an unsolvable problem.

Among other therapy activities that the patient can continue are doing or reading dysfunctional thought records, listing accomplishments, setting specific goals, making plans to reduce avoidance, graded-exposure tasks, identifying costs and benefits of behaviors, self-monitoring, activity scheduling, and posting reminders containing revised beliefs or adaptive cognitions.

A rationale for continuing such self-directed therapeutic tasks will need to be given. Any objections to putting forth time and effort on these tasks, such as, "I shouldn't have to work this hard" or "This is too much of an effort," will need to be dealt with before therapy ends. The costs and benefits of such efforts can be explored with the patient. The advantages of making self-therapy a priority, even when feeling well, need to be stressed. The analogous situation of medical patients ceasing to take necessary long-term medication when feeling better can be used to underscore this point. Also, the evidence that old habits tend to return if replacement habits are not practiced regularly can be cited.

To formalize these maintenance efforts, patients can set a daily or weekly appointment with themselves, modeled on their actual therapy sessions. They can put aside 30 to 60 minutes for these sessions on a regular basis, for example, every day, week, or month. The act of making this time available tends by itself to make the patient's emotional state a priority. Within the self-therapy session the patient can follow the format below (J. S. Beck, 1994):

1. Set an agenda (What do I need to think about?).
2. Review any homework (What have I learned?).
3. Review the week (What positive/negative things happened? How could I have handled things better? What tools did I use?).
4. Engage in self-monitoring (How am I doing with depression, anxiety, or specific symptoms or problems?).
5. Target problems (What problems do I need to work on? What exactly is going on? What are the triggers, my thoughts and feelings? What can I do?).
6. Set new homework (What can I do to follow up on today's work?).
7. Set up a future appointment (How soon should I do this again?).

The therapist can also provide the patient with written assignments in order to facilitate the self-therapy. Or the patient can imagine sessions with the therapist in order to review the therapist's manner of conducting the session. Essentially, the patient is role-playing the therapist and this facilitates self-questioning and intervention.

Another method of consolidating skills is to have the former patient teach the skills to someone else. This can be done by arranging for the former patient to co-lead a cognitive-behavioral group (e.g., be a co-leader in a support group for anxious individuals) or to help a friend or family member with emotional problems using cognitive-behavioral methods. It might also be helpful in this regard to encourage certain former patients to write an article on anxiety, depression, or other topics; to give interviews to the local media; or to present through a speakers' bureau on these topics. All of these involve practice and generalization and so facilitate maintenance and relapse-prevention.

Specifying the Steps in Relapse-Prevention. It is important throughout the later phases of therapy to regularly review with patients the specific steps involved in relapse-prevention. When they find themselves slipping back, depressed and anxious patients who have been working on maintenance and relapse-prevention can be encouraged to remember to

1. Stop whatever they are doing.
2. Examine the situation that is contributing to their affective shift.
3. Identify the automatic thoughts that are mediating the situation-affect link.

Having carried out such an analysis, patients can then be encouraged to carry out some specific steps to attempt to change (a) the situation (including their own or someone else's behavior) using problem-solving techniques; (b) their thoughts using well-practiced cognitive techniques; or (c) their affective state using methods like relaxation, exercise, or medication. In the later stages of therapy, the goal should be to have patients carry out an analysis of what is going on when problems arise, decide what their targets for change are, and then put into practice specific strategies to achieve these targets. Patients who learn how to do this are well on their way to becoming their own therapist, and such efforts should be facilitated and reinforced at this stage of therapy.

Lifestyle Change. At this point of therapy, there should also be a focus on issues relating to lifestyle and lifestyle balance. Over and above identifying and preparing for specific high-risk situations, as outlined earlier, patients should be encouraged to look at their life situations and how these might be altered or better balanced to produce greater emotional stability. Because numerous studies demonstrate the impact of environmental factors on depression and anxiety, Miller (1984) points out that these issues may also impede continued therapeutic progress if attention is not focused on changing the patient's environment. Changes in life areas such as (a) work (getting or leaving a job, reducing hours), (b) social life (increasing or decreasing social activity, making new friends, severing relations with nonsupportive, critical friends), (c) personal relationships (ending, changing, initiating new relationships), and (d) living situations (changing accommodations) may be an important part of continued recovery and maintenance.

Balancing lifestyle (Marlatt & Gordon, 1985) involves examining the extent to which a patient's daily activities contain a sufficient pattern of good coping strategies to offset the demands or stressors placed on the individual. Imbalances between work/duty and play/pleasure and between doing things for other people (family, friends) and doing things for oneself can be examined in collaboration with the patient. The consequences of such imbalances for this individual can be explored using a costs-benefits analysis, and concrete plans to alter existing patterns can be made. A time analysis (see Appendix E, p. 69) can be used to demonstrate imbalances to the patient and also to plan a different and more healthy division of time.

For those patients in demanding, high-stress life situations, time-management techniques and general strategies for reducing stress can be incorporated into this phase of therapy. It may be helpful to assess patients' level of daily hassles, using the Hassles Scale (Kanner et al., 1987), as well as to assess uplifts or positive experiences, using the uplifts scale (Kanner et al., 1987) or the

Pleasant Events Scale (Lewinsohn & Graf, 1973), and then to examine ways to reduce the former and increase the latter. In addition, developing a balance between shoulds (external demands) and wants (activities engaged in for pleasure or self-fulfillment) is likely to be important in developing a healthier lifestyle and promoting sustained recovery (Marlatt & Gordon, 1985). Many patients will need to be encouraged to plan or schedule periods of time for pleasurable activities or for "looking after themselves" in the same way that they plan or schedule tasks and chores. This will help make their own needs/wants a higher priority than they may have previously been in their lives.

Reviewing Post-Discharge Plans. One last and obvious focus of the later stages of therapy is that of reviewing the patient's post-termination plans. This should include exploring with patients (a) their self-directed plans for maintenance, including joining support groups, (b) any post-discharge plans to continue therapy or counseling in this setting or elsewhere, (c) the necessity for booster sessions and how exactly these will be set up, if they become necessary, and (d) under what circumstances patients should re-enter active treatment, as distinct from merely seeking booster sessions. Any negative or dysfunctional thoughts the patient has about having booster sessions or making contact with the therapist again after therapy is over can be elicited at this stage, for example, "I wouldn't want to bother you."

Self-Efficacy Enhancement. All of the previously referenced therapeutic efforts in the different phases of active therapy can be seen as "self-efficacy enhancement strategies" (Marlatt & Gordon, 1985). The goal of efficacy enhancement is to facilitate a change in the patients' self-image so that they see themselves as victors not victims, as able to problem solve and take control rather than to become helpless. It is hoped that by utilizing these methods, the patient will see himself or herself as being in possession of resources to maintain progress and prevent or recover from slip-backs rather than as a passive carrier of a disease that is likely to recur and over which the sufferer has no control. Marlatt and Gordon (1985) contend that the best methods to promote self-efficacy involve (a) the therapist and patient collaborating in an active therapy program, (b) a strong emphasis in therapy on skill-acquisition, (c) a focus on helping the patient view recovery and relapse as a process or journey with several stages rather than an outcome, and (d) the use of therapy sessions to provide patients with regular opportunities to practice and receive feedback about their performance and progress.

Use of Metaphors and Analogies. All of the preceding strategies are applicable to individual cognitive-behavioral treatment on an inpatient or outpatient basis. They can also be used in group therapy in both inpatient and outpatient settings. Of course, the procedures and content can be modified for different formats and settings. In both inpatient and outpatient groups, several sessions can be devoted to discharge planning and relapse-prevention. In the group setting, metaphors or analogies used in individual therapy can be even more powerful as means of creating the appropriate cognitive set for patients' use of maintenance and relapse-prevention strategies on their own after termination.

The metaphor of recovery as a road or journey can be very helpful to illustrate to group members or individual patients the skills and techniques outlined previously. For example, before discharge, a group or individual can be told:

If you think of the process of sustained recovery as being like a long journey, this will help you realize that, although recovery or maintenance may take time and effort, you will eventually get to your destination. Now, just like on a journey, the first thing to be decided is your destination. Similarly, in terms of your emotional health or problems, what do you ultimately want to achieve? (Get individual or group to answer this question and record it.) On a long journey you may have to plan several stages, places you would stop overnight or take a break. What are your shorter term goals? Where do you want to be in 1 month, 3 months, 1 year? (Get the group or individual to answer and record this.) Setting out on a journey, you have a departure point, for example, home, overnight stop, and so on. Where are you starting from? Where are you in terms of solving the problems you have? (Ask individual or group to answer and record this.) On a car journey, you would probably check that you had the right tools for the journey, for example, a jack to change a tire, a flashlight, and so forth. What are the tools/skills that you bring with you on your journey? (Ask individual or group to answer and record this.) When you are driving, there are certain things to look out for which warn you that you might break down, for example, oil light, fuel light, knocking noise from the engine, and so on. What are early warning signs suggesting that you are slipping back emotionally which you need to pay attention to? (Ask individual or group to answer and record this.) On a road journey there are a number of possible hazards which you need to be aware of and then take appropriate corrective action, for example, other drivers' behavior or bad road conditions which prompt you to slow down and be more vigilant. Likewise, there are certain high-risk situations in terms of relapse that you need to recognize and prepare for. What are these situations for you? (Get individual or group to answer and record this.) Lastly, it is possible on a journey that your car may break down or you may take a wrong turn. At this point, you need to be a problem solver rather than to get upset and incapacitated; for example, call someone to help rather than angrily kick the stranded car. Though you may never have to use it, it will be helpful for you to have a plan if you have some recurrence of symptoms or problems. What is your emergency plan in the event of a lapse that will get you back on your journey? (Get individual or group to answer and record this.)

This extended metaphor can be adapted or elaborated for certain formats or patient populations. Other appropriate analogies or metaphors pertaining to relapse and recovery can also be incorporated into relapse-prevention work at different stages of therapy (Marlatt & Gordon, 1985).

FOLLOW-UP/AFTER-CARE ACTIVITIES

After the termination of formal therapy, there are a number of ways in which continued progress can be facilitated, including booster sessions and refresher groups which will be discussed in more detail below. Other follow-up strategies include self-therapy sessions (as described earlier) and the use of such resources as family and friends, as well as other community-based resources including churches, day treatment centers, and support groups.

Booster Sessions. In the later phase of active therapy, the therapist often fades therapy sessions so that the sessions become less frequent or of shorter duration. The reduction in frequency and/or duration of therapy sessions encourages the patient to increase his or her coping efforts and take more responsibility for solving problems or dealing with emotional distress. Following the end of the acute phase of therapy, the patient and therapist may decide collaboratively to set up booster sessions for a specified or as-needed follow-up period. Although research studies have not demonstrated superior clinical outcome with the use of booster sessions (Baker & Wilson, 1985), there would seem to be a number of advantages to conducting booster sessions:

1. If booster sessions are spaced out or infrequent, patients may be encouraged to cope with difficulties on their own first, but with the knowledge that they can discuss these efforts in the next booster session and receive suggestions and feedback.
2. Booster sessions give some continuity to treatment and also reinforce the concept of recovery as being a long-term process of coping and dealing with problems as they arise.
3. Patients may be more likely to continue maintenance efforts due to increased accountability, as well as the reinforcement ensuing from therapist contact.
4. Booster sessions allow the therapist an opportunity to monitor the patient's progress and to take action, if necessary (e.g., increase the frequency of sessions, consider medication changes).

A good rationale needs to be given to the patient for booster sessions that incorporates some of the previous advantages. Booster sessions can be carried out face-to-face (in individual, couple, or group formats) or by telephone. If other preferred methods are impossible, the patient and therapist in unusual circumstances might even use tapes or letters to continue contact in the after-care phase. In addition to booster sessions, some continued contact by the therapist with significant others (with the patient's permission) might be used to monitor the patient's progress.

Booster sessions can be set up in a number of ways:

1. They can be on a regular schedule for a prescribed period of time (e.g., every month or 3 months for 2 years).
2. They can be on a faded schedule (e.g., monthly, then trimonthly, then 6-monthly).
3. They can be scheduled on an "as-needed" basis (in which case they may be crisis-driven and scheduled after other strategies have been tried and failed).

Formal re-entry into treatment or a change in the frequency or format of booster sessions can be made at any time in the light of the therapist and patient's assessment of what is needed. Likewise, face-to-face and telephone contact can be used in a manner that best meets the needs of the patient. In some instances, it may be decided that sessions will be scheduled with the option to cancel if the patient feels he or she is doing well or requires only a briefer telephone review of progress rather than a full booster session. In some cases, it may be important to stress to the patient that he or she should come for booster sessions even if he or she doesn't think it is necessary. Even when the patient is feeling well, he or she can be encouraged to see these sessions as a preventive measure in the way that a medical checkup is helpful.

To maximize the benefits to patients, it is important that booster sessions be well structured and that the patient actively prepare for the session. Patients can be given some guidelines before therapy ends as to how to maximize the value of these sessions. They can be encouraged to develop a plan for booster sessions and to bring items for the agenda, writing down material so they will not forget in the longer intervals between these sessions. Items to discuss in the session might be generated by asking themselves the following questions (J. S. Beck, 1994):

- What has gone well for me since the last booster session?
- What problems have arisen recently and how did I handle them?
- How could I have coped better?
- What problems could arise in the near future or before my next booster session?
- What have I done to maintain my progress after therapy?
- What gets in the way of maintaining my skills?
- What else might I do?
- What goals do I have for myself?
- What specific plans do I have to achieve these?
- What issues do I want to discuss with my therapist over and above the problems I have identified here?

The use of individual or group booster sessions will involve all of the strategies outlined earlier to promote maintenance, such as anticipating high-risk situations, developing "emergency procedures," and training in detection of early warning signs of relapse. Booster sessions will most typically be done on an individual basis. However, in the case of closed-ended cognitive-behavioral groups, booster sessions can also be set up for the group as a whole to maintain progress and prevent relapse.

Group Refresher Sessions. An alternative to the type of booster sessions described earlier that appears to have great potential in terms of maintenance and relapse-prevention and is cost-effective in terms of therapist time is the strategy of having "refresher sessions" for groups of former patients. This differs from group therapy booster sessions in that the emphasis is not on therapy per se as much as on education or skill-consolidation. Such sessions can in fact be set up and promoted as workshops or seminars for former patients. A relatively homogenous group of patients, each of whom had received cognitive-behavioral therapy for their specific problems, can be brought together for refresher sessions in which the methods of cognitive-behavioral therapy, rather than participants' problems, are focused on.

In the course of interviewing former patients for a 5-year follow-up study of depressed outpatients (Ludgate, 1991), a significant number of these individuals reported that they felt they could have benefited from a cognitive therapy refresher or maintenance group led by a therapist at regular intervals. Some of these former patients were of the opinion that, had such sessions been available, they may not have needed to re-enter therapy when symptoms recurred. The idea of such after-care workshops arose out of this observation, combined with the author's interest in secondary and tertiary prevention.

In actual clinical practice, these sessions could be offered to all former patients who had participated in individual or group cognitive-behavior therapy. This may be particularly beneficial and cost-effective in large practices or hospital and clinic settings. It has to be kept in mind that these sessions are not a substitute for therapy. This should be stressed in materials describing these sessions (see Appendix F, p. 71).

These seminars or workshops are intended to be refresher sessions with an explicitly educational focus. They can be a cost-effective way of maintaining progress in some patients, while at the same time allowing the therapist to keep abreast of former patients' progress.

The session content might revolve around

1. Reviewing general cognitive-behavioral skills.
2. Reviewing relapse-prevention strategies.
3. Facilitating goal-setting and planning by each participant.
4. Discussing topics suggested by participants (e.g., self-esteem, procrastination, approval-seeking).

A sample agenda for a 1-day refresher session is included in Appendix G (p. 73).

All former patients or only specially selected former patients can be contacted and informed of upcoming refresher sessions (see

Appendix F, p. 71). In addition, current patients who are nearing discharge can be informed of this after-care option. These sessions can also be used by former patients on an as-needed basis. They can be offered regularly on either a monthly or tri-monthly basis. In some cases, patients may still be attending regular therapy sessions. This is not an exclusionary criterion, providing a framework is given to both the therapist and patient as to how these sessions relate to ongoing therapy. In some cases, recommendations for re-instatement of formal therapy may be made during these sessions. The opportunity afforded to the therapist to monitor a large number of former patients' progress and to take action, if necessary, is another advantage of these sessions.

With the appropriate safeguards and with the participants' permission, significant others could also attend these sessions or possibly have educational, maintenance-focused seminars or workshops of their own.

The distinctive features of this approach, which can be incorporated into both hospital-based and outpatient cognitive therapy programs, are as follows:

1. An emphasis on educational skill-building and skill-consolidation
2. The potential involvement of many former patients (some of whom would possibly not re-enter therapy on an as-needed basis)
3. The provision of assistance not only to those former patients who have setbacks, but also to those who want to work on maintenance
4. The high degree to which former patients can control and contribute to the content of the agenda
5. The focus on general methods and strategies that can apply to all participants across a wide variety of situations rather than an individual or group therapy focus
6. The provision of a strong message to former patients that they are cognitive-behavior therapy graduates returning for a "tune-up" or refresher session with the consequent avoid-

ance of the negative cognitions sometimes associated with a return to formal therapy

SPECIFIC DIFFICULTIES IN MAINTAINING TREATMENT GAINS AND PREVENTING RELAPSE

In this section, potential problems for both the therapist and patient in working on maintenance and relapse-prevention will be identified. Possible solutions and strategies to deal with these will be outlined.

THE PATIENT WHO DOES NOT WANT TO END THERAPY

It is important for the therapist to adequately conceptualize this problem and, in particular, to ascertain the patient's cognitions on the meaning of termination. The patient's predictions about what will happen when therapy ends and his or her feelings about the end of the relationship need to be explored. For some patients who are fearful of slipping back after termination, spacing sessions or booster sessions can be set up as an experiment to test out such hypotheses. Also, the patient's own skills and self-efficacy can be reviewed when the patient believes that the therapist is necessary for continued recovery. Generally, the task will be to substitute the patient's own efforts, social network, and support system for regular therapy and to get the patient to see these as helpful in his or her recovery.

THE OVERLY DEPENDENT PATIENT WHO DOES NOT TAKE AN ACTIVE PART IN THERAPY

As pointed out earlier, increasing patients' activity level as therapy progresses is an important aspect of developing a mental set towards self-directed maintenance and relapse-prevention after therapy. Some patients will be resistant to this and will want the therapist to "do it for them." The therapist needs to be alert to this problem and should not be seduced by the flattering implication that he or she has all the answers. Cognitions such as, "I can't manage on my own" or "My therapist should tell me what to do" need to be brought into the open and dealt with as any dysfunctional thoughts would be.

A good rationale for a high level of patient activity should be given throughout therapy. Likewise, the self-help nature of cognitive-behavior therapy should be made very explicit, and the cost and benefits of this approach versus therapy "being done to the patient" need to be explored. Guided discovery should be used at all possible opportunities, and the patient should be encouraged to set agendas and come up with homework assignments. Naturally, the patient should be strongly reinforced for these and any other independent behaviors. Offering choices and alternatives to the patient as often as possible, getting the patient's feedback at each step in therapy, and asking open-ended rather than closed-ended questions will all foster more patient involvement in therapy.

THE PATIENT WHO RELAPSES QUICKLY AFTER TERMINATION

The therapist's task here is to conceptualize and help the patient understand the relapse process. Other important objectives are to help restructure the meaning of the relapse, to encourage the patient to apply all of his or her coping skills appropriately, to determine the need for more therapy sessions or medication, and, most importantly, to re-install a sense of self-efficacy in the patient who is discouraged and demoralized. Often such patients will need to be helped to see that slipping back or experiencing some symptom recurrence is not so much the problem as how they react to this experience. Informing the patient that relapse is not infrequent after termination, especially in inpatients or outpatients who have been in therapy for a long time, may be useful in getting the patient to put this in perspective. It will also be helpful to provide an explanation of how this lapse occurred in the patient's case, particularly if this explanation stresses external factors rather than personal deficits in the patient.

THE PATIENT WHO GETS DISCOURAGED
FOLLOWING RELAPSE OR DUE TO THE
AMOUNT OF EFFORT NEEDED FOR MAINTENANCE

In such cases, the therapist should carefully explore the patient's cognitions and expectations regarding recovery and relapse. Patients may have unrealistic expectations, such as, "I am now over my depression and will never feel bad again" or "It shouldn't be this hard." Patients who expect their progress to be linear may become self-pitying, angry, or discouraged when negative feelings recur and, thus, may become unable to problem solve. Some patients will also expect that negative thoughts will not re-emerge after therapy or that they will always be able to combat them quickly and effectively. A win-win situation can be set up by the therapist by giving the patient the following message: "Old habits, such as certain negative thoughts, are likely to recur. If you can deal with them successfully, this is the best outcome. But if you cannot, this will also be very helpful as it will give some useful information on the kind of thinking that keeps you depressed, which can then be worked on in booster sessions or at other times when you are less distressed."

The therapist needs to watch out for perfectionistic or defeatist attitudes in patients who respond to the re-emergence of negative thoughts or unpleasant affect states with either hopelessness or anger (often towards themselves). Such patients need to be shown how self-defeating these responses are in contrast to a problem-solving approach. A cost-benefit analysis that contrasts continuing to work on one's problems versus giving up can be carried out at this point in an attempt to get the patient to actively decide to continue his or her maintenance work rather than to give up.

It is also necessary to prepare the patient for situations like the above by letting him or her know that the ability to reduce negative feelings and to answer negative thoughts will take time and a good deal of practice. The analogy can be made with other skills familiar to the patient, for example, learning to drive or play a sport. The patient can be told, "When you first try this (particular skill/activity), you have to work very hard in a self-conscious way to avoid making mistakes. You may get temporarily distressed by anything difficult or unusual at this point. Later, with practice, you will be able to deal more easily with harder situations, and you will also find that your responses become more automatic. The difficulties and mistakes made earlier are actually a chance to practice and learn."

THE PATIENT WHO DOES NOT WANT TO
FOLLOW MEDICATION RECOMMENDATIONS

Some patients receiving cognitive-behavior therapy will either be on psychotropic medication or are being withdrawn from pharmacological agents, especially antianxiety agents like benzodiazepines. Patients may be reluctant to either initiate taking medication or to continue on a medication maintenance regime which may be indicated in view of their diagnosis or history. Alternatively, patients may be reluctant to come off medication, even with a medically supervised, gradual, tapering-off program. The important issue here for the therapist is to conceptualize the difficulty in cognitive-behavioral terms. It may be that the patient is having practical difficulties withdrawing from or starting medications, but more significantly, he or she may have strong beliefs about medication, such as, "I will become an addict if I start taking any medication for more than a short time" or "I can't make it without my pills; I just know my panic attacks will come right back." A number of therapeutic methods will be helpful here. The patient can be asked to examine the evidence for these thoughts and to consider alternative perspectives or views of the situation. The patient's worst fears can be identified, and he or she can be helped to imagine coping in this situation. Plans can be set up for future monitoring of thoughts, feelings, and sensations relevant to medication use, and some re-education concerning side-effects and dependence can also be carried out.

THE PATIENT WHO STOPS
WORKING ON MAINTENANCE
ONCE SYMPTOMS ARE REDUCED

Here again it is important to conceptualize the difficulty and explore cognitions and reasons for noncompliance. The therapist should emphasize that it is always the patient's choice whether to continue or not, but a cost-benefit analysis can be carried out to explore the possible consequences of not continuing maintenance work. It is also important to discuss with the patient his or her priorities, especially how high maintenance of emotional health is on his or her priority list.

The patient may need help in making maintenance and relapse-prevention a priority. An analogy can be made to the fact that people find the time to walk daily if they have a heart condition requiring this kind of exercise. The patient needs to be given a rationale for putting forth effort as a preventive measure similar to brushing his or her teeth to prevent cavities in the future. It is also a good idea to acknowledge to the patient that he or she may not want to make the effort. Although this is natural, it is irrelevant because the real question is whether it is worth it. Examples of things people do for certain benefits, while preferring not to, such as going to the dentist, can be used here. The notion that action leads to motivation (Burns, 1981) rather than the other way around, as commonly believed, is also a useful strategy to adopt here.

THE PATIENT WHO HAS EXCESSIVE LIFE STRESS IN THE THERAPY OR AFTER-CARE PHASE

As mentioned earlier, life stress is often associated with relapse in depressed and anxious patients, especially when patients have a low sense of self-efficacy. The emphasis here should be on anticipating, where possible, upcoming stressors, preparing the patient by reviewing emergency procedures, and facilitating regular rehearsal and practice of general problem solving and self-management skills. One common therapeutic pitfall here is that the therapist becomes too supportive and gets inappropriately enmeshed in the patient's view of how bad things are.

It is important to realize that even when the patient's situation is realistically aversive or unpleasant, whenever there is severe emotional distress, it is to be expected that there will be some distortions in his or her thinking about these situations. The therapist, while acknowledging the reality of the situation, should also look for the distorted thinking and, in particular, help the patient to distinguish exaggerated conclusions ("I'm unlovable") from the actual events themselves ("My husband told me he didn't love me anymore"). The patient can be helped to examine how other people in the same aversive situation manage to cope effectively and not get depressed. They may also be encouraged to recall similar situations that they successfully coped with in the past and to identify what skills they used then. The therapist can also explore whether the situation can be changed or will always remain the same. If the situation is realistically stressful but could possibly be changed (e.g., leaving an abusive relationship), it will be helpful to identify and work on thoughts that prevent the patient from attempting to change the situation.

Generally, trouble-shooting here involves a good conceptualization of the difficulty, the role played by the patient's cognitions, and the re-introduction of effective problem-solving methods.

THE PATIENT WHO SEES RECOVERY OR RELAPSE IN ALL-OR-NOTHING TERMS

Some patients, as well as having somewhat unrealistic expectations about the course of their disorder or recovery, will also see related situations in a black-and-white or all-or-nothing way. If they experience some symptom recurrence, they will have cognitions such as, "I'm just back to square one" with the resultant belief that "I can now do nothing except go back to the clinic or hospital."

All-or-nothing thinking, in combination with an external attributional style regarding change, is particularly destructive in terms of hopelessness. The belief that any lapse constitutes complete failure leads to the patient's ceasing any efforts to help himself or herself and a resignation to a deteriorating course predicted by the belief system. The therapist needs to actively challenge this dichotomous thinking and encourage the patient to recognize small and subtle changes.

In the event of a setback, it is important to get the patient to examine exactly how far he or she has slipped back relative to the start of treatment and to see what was in any way positive in his or her response ("I didn't run from the store this time"), as well as what was negative in his or her response ("I got a severe panic attack"). Lastly, for such patients, a key element in getting them back on track is helping them to see relapse not as a single event, but as a process with choice points where they, with the therapist's help, can intervene.

THE AXIS II PATIENT WHO HAS A REACTIVATION OF DYSFUNCTIONAL SCHEMA

This will often be triggered by stressful life events. Critical incidents which bear on the belief system, for example, the departure of a spouse in a patient who believes "I must have a man to survive," will trigger the re-emergence of this schema with its associated specific cognitions ("I'm falling apart"), affect (panic, anger), and behavior (clinging to family members or over-dependence on the therapist). Although the therapist will use crisis-intervention and affect-reduction techniques to help the acutely distressed patient function better, in many cases this will only be the first stage and will need to be followed by some schema work. Here, as in all situations involving setbacks, conceptualizing the relapse or crisis episode will be essential.

Following this, the therapist can help the patient to recognize common themes in this situation and others worked on earlier in therapy (e.g., a belief such as, "I can't make it alone"). Methods used earlier to deal with these beliefs can then be re-introduced and the patient encouraged to continue maintenance work to re-inforce new, revised beliefs (e.g., recording accomplishments that are related to independence and self-reliance). In Axis II patients, such setbacks can often be predicted in the light of the patient's history and some work can be done in preparation for such events. Giving patients realistic expectations regarding the risk of this is important.

Following the therapeutic efforts mentioned here, it is vital to plan and get the patient to carry out daily self-directed therapy on residual dysfunctional beliefs or schemas. Journal keeping; cost-benefit analysis of these beliefs; the downward arrow method

(Burns, 1981); historical review of such beliefs (McKay & Fanning, 1991); and reading, practicing, and acting on new beliefs may all be helpful ways to achieve this.

GENERAL GUIDELINES FOR THERAPISTS WORKING WITH PATIENTS WHO RELAPSE

KEEP A PROBLEM-SOLVING ATTITUDE

When problems arise, such as frequent relapses or problems motivating the patient to work at maintenance, it will be best if the difficulty can be specified precisely, conceptualized, and possible solutions generated, evaluated, and tried out. Attempts at problem solving done collaboratively with the patient provide a good model for the patient to observe and try out on his or her own in the future, if necessary. Particularly in cases where there are frequent crises, it will be important to keep longer term goals in mind and to stick to a general strategy even when being obliged to deal with specific crises or putting out "brush fires."

AVOID LABELING OR STEREOTYPING THE PATIENT

Many patients, owing to the nature of their problems, will provide strenuous challenges to the therapist or in some cases with inpatients, to the entire treatment team. In such cases, it is important to bear in mind that the patient is not the problem - his or her difficulties and distress are the problem. Labeling or stereotyping the patient as "resistant," "difficult," or "self-defeating" only serves to prevent a thorough analysis of what factors (e.g., beliefs, distortions in thinking) are leading the patient to act in a particular way.

Blaming the patient or external factors solely is both antitherapeutic and does not promote the collaboration and problem-solving focus so important to cognitive-behavior therapy. In addition, when the patient is seen as the problem, a filtering out of the patient's assets and strengths often occurs and potential solutions are often ignored.

PERSIST WITH THE MODEL WHEN
SERIOUS PROBLEMS ARISE

Some therapists in situations where treatment gains are not maintained or relapse has occurred are prone to give up on the therapy they have been conducting. They may adopt a different therapy model because of their own discouragement rather than because there is a good rationale for this shift in emphasis. This will be confusing to the patient and may serve to reinforce the belief that this therapy has not worked for him or her. A careful analysis should be made of why the individual is experiencing continued problems and a problem-solving attitude adopted to see what needs to be done.

If indicated, other treatment options which follow from this analysis should be considered (e.g., the use of medication or family approaches) and a good rationale given to the patient to avoid confusion. Other approaches that supplement cognitive-behavioral therapy should be considered before a completely different treatment option is initiated. A related problem is when therapists do not abandon the model, as such, but become less active and more supportive when the patient relapses in the belief that a less directive approach is needed. It may be that this is precisely the time when the therapist needs to increase both patient and therapist activity level and to engage in aggressive problem solving rather than to buy into the patient's distorted view of reality and to indulge in joining with the patient in a self-pitying, "it really is awful" attitude.

IDENTIFY AND DEAL
WITH THERAPIST
DYSFUNCTIONAL COGNITIONS

Many of the situations outlined earlier in which obstacles to maintenance and relapse-prevention arise may create some demoralization and distress in the therapist as well as the patient. In such situations, it is particularly important that the therapist be aware of his or her dysfunctional cognitions, for example, "This patient has relapsed so I'm inadequate as a therapist," or "The patient should try harder, considering all the effort I've put in."

When patients relapse, dysfunctional beliefs that mediate emotional reactions like anxiety, depression, and anger in the therapist should be examined and responded to. The same methods used to help patients identify and challenge thoughts can be applied when the therapist experiences strong negative emotions concerning a patient's lack of progress. Therapists need to learn not to take relapse or lack of progress personally, but to look for possible reasons for this and attempt to work on these in a problem-solving way.

BE REALISTIC IN EXPECTATIONS

In the same way that patients often have unrealistic expectations concerning treatment which may set them up for disappointment, therapists may also hold unrealistic and dysfunctional expectations concerning patients, themselves, or the kind of therapy they do. In particular, it is important that the therapist adjust his or her expectations to a realistic level (without giving up hope) with certain patients who have long histories, chronic disorders, Axis II diagnoses, and so on. What is involved here is not giving up hope for a particular patient, but having a realistic time frame and expecting setbacks and obstacles to progress in therapy. A good case conceptualization, as Persons (1989) points out, will allow the therapist to predict obstacles and setbacks in advance and not become demoralized or frustrated.

In addition to setting realistic targets (e.g., helping a borderline patient to reduce or rechannel self-destructive impulses rather than get rid of these impulses completely) the therapist should look for ways to measure small changes toward these goals in an effort to reinforce both the patient's and therapist's efforts and to prevent overgeneralizing ("This patient always acts out") or all-or-nothing thinking ("He/She is making no progress with the problem of impulsivity").

SEEK SUPPORT OR ADVICE

Many therapists work in considerable isolation, either geographically or personally. Where this is the case and the therapist has a number of patients who have relapsed or are not doing well for whatever reason, some degree of therapist stress is probably inevitable. In addition to the strategies for dealing with these situations outlined above, it may also be important for the therapist to seek support from peers. Psychotherapy can be a lonely profession because therapists are often reluctant to "burden" family or friends with their professional concerns. Provisions for formal or informal supervision on a group or individual basis may be helpful, as will attendance at workshops and conferences related to work in which the therapist is engaged. Taking the initiative in seeking support, advice, or help related to clinical impasses often requires the therapist to successfully combat dysfunctional cognitions, such as, "I should be able to deal with this myself," or "They may think I'm inadequate." Formal or informal consultations with colleagues or peers also may often help considerably. In other cases, therapists may need to examine other stress-reducing options, such as revising expectations, modifying beliefs, taking more time off, regular exercise, better leisure-planning, lifestyle modification, or entering therapy themselves.

MYTHS REGARDING RELAPSE

Chiauzzi (1992) outlines some myths about relapse in addictive disorders treatment that can stall treatment or contribute to relapse. These are equally applicable to depression. These myths can be held by the therapist, the patient, or the patient's family. Some of the most common are

- Relapse is a totally unpredictable process, even after the fact.
- Relapse begins with the first symptom reccurence or return to maladaptive behavior.
- Relapse results from a lack of willpower.
- People decide consciously that they want to relapse and do so for secondary gain.
- Relapse means failure.
- Relapse negates any growth made up to that point.
- Relapsers will only be motivated to re-enter treatment or work on their problems when they hit "rock bottom."

Therapists who subscribe to any of these notions need to work on their own dysfunctional cognitions in order to be of better service to their emotionally distressed patients. Efforts to elicit such distorted beliefs from patients and their families is likely to be helpful in setting the stage for the development of a more adaptive cognitive set that will, in turn, enable the patient to consolidate or re-learn self-management skills in order to maintain treatment gains and prevent future relapses.

SUMMARY

Cognitive behavior therapy has several important characteristics that may help to facilitate maintenance of treatment gains and prevent relapse in emotionally distressed patients. These include:

- the high degree of patient activity, including planning and completing intersession assignments
- the increasing level of patient responsibility for session content and for the implementation of cognitive-behavioral strategies as therapy proceeds
- the self-help focus and collaborative nature of this therapy
- the acquisition of general skills to control emotional disturbance which can be used in the event of symptom recurrence
- the targeting of vulnerability factors such as dysfunctional attitudes and attributional style.

Research studies indicate that emotionally distressed patients who are treated with cognitive behavior therapy are afforded some prophylaxis against relapse. However, despite these encouraging findings, a significant percentage of cognitive behavior therapy patients will experience a recurrence of symptoms. A more systematic application of effective cognitive-behavioral strategies that clearly target maintenance and relapse-prevention is required to help these patients.

Specific procedures that the therapist can use during therapy to promote maintenance and prevent relapse include the following:

- assessing risk factors in each patient and tailoring therapy to focus on these issues
- graphing the patient's progress and providing frequent reviews of skills acquired
- anticipating and preparing the patient for termination
- emphasizing the goal of therapy as the patient becoming his or her own therapist
- overlearning of skills
- generalizing of acquired skills to new or future problem situations
- focusing on schema change and targeting vulnerability factors
- dealing with Axis II issues and stressful life events
- promoting internal attributions of change
- increasing patient activity and responsibility as therapy proceeds to foster self-efficacy
- fading of therapy session frequency or duration later in therapy
- educating the patient regarding relapse and recovery
- exploring the meaning of lapses or setbacks
- distinguishing between a lapse and a full relapse
- anticipating negative thoughts about setbacks and promoting more adaptive thinking
- recognizing early warning signals of relapse
- anticipating and planning for high-risk situations
- creating an emergency plan for setbacks in collaboration with the patient
- planning a self-therapy program or maintenance plan
- promoting lifestyle change to reinforce therapy gains
- enlisting significant others to support the patient's maintenance activities

Specific activities that may prove beneficial to the patient in the after-care phase include:

- following a self-directed maintenance plan
- attending group "refresher" sessions for former patients
- scheduling booster sessions

- receiving maintenance or continuation therapy (using pharmacotherapy and/or psychotherapy) after symptomatic relief has occurred

APPENDICES

APPENDIX A:
SELF-MONITORING CHART*

Beck
Depression
Inventory
Score
(BDI)

65 _____

60 _____

55 _____

50 _____

45 _____

40 _____

35 _____

30 _____

25 _____

20 _____

15 _____

10 _____

5 _____

0 _____

Date of
Self-Assessment

*Note: The same chart can be used to monitor anxiety using the Beck Anxiety Inventory.

APPENDIX B:
GENERAL THOUGHT-TESTING PROCEDURE

Step 1

What are the negative thoughts contributing to my emotional shift? How much do I believe each of these (0%-100%)?

Thoughts   *% Belief*

_____   _____

_____   _____

_____   _____

Step 2

What thinking errors or distortions am I making?

_____

_____

Step 3

What is the evidence for these thoughts?

Evidence for   *Evidence against*

_____   _____

_____   _____

_____   _____

_____   _____

Step 4

What alternative views are there?

_____

_____

_____

Step 5

What can I do to test my thinking or to work on the problem?

_____

_____

_____

Step 6

In the light of the preceding, what are more realistic thoughts I can substitute for those in Step 1?

_____

_____

_____

APPENDIX C:
GENERAL PROBLEM-SOLVING PROCEDURE

Step 1

Define the problem and your goal in this situation in concrete terms.

The problem is _____.
My goal in this situation is _____
_____.

Step 2

Generate as many solutions as possible. Brainstorm from your own past experience and from imagining how others might attempt to solve this problem. Consider a wide range of possible options.

Possible Solutions	Pros	Cons	Rank

Step 3

Evaluate the pros and cons of each proposed solution and rank them from most promising to least promising solution.

Step 4

Try out the highest ranked solution. Make a concrete plan regarding how you will put this into action and follow through on the plan.

My action plan is _____

_____

_____

Step 5

Reconsider the original problem in the light of what happened when this solution was attempted. If necessary, try out other solutions.

APPENDIX D:
EARLY WARNING SIGNS OF RELAPSE

Put a check opposite any of the following symptoms you have recently experienced.

___ Sleep disturbance
___ Appetite disturbance
___ Concentration/Short-term memory problems
___ Suicidal thoughts/Feelings of hopelessness
___ Excessive self-criticism/Feelings of worthlessness
___ Loss of motivation
___ Social withdrawal
___ Inability to make decisions
___ Apathy and indifference
___ Loss of energy
___ Excessive guilt/Brooding about the past
___ Agitation
___ Significant mood changes
___ Anxiety or panic attacks
___ Decreased productivity
___ Helplessness/Feelings of having no control
___ Excessive anger
___ Apprehensiveness/Fearfulness
___ Negative thinking
___ Loss of interest
___ Difficulty feeling pleasure
___ Other incapacitating symptoms not listed above
    Please specify _____
    _____
    _____
    _____
    _____

APPENDIX E:
LIFESTYLE BALANCE

Estimate the percentage of time you currently spend on the following activities, and then indicate the percentage of time you would like to spend on each.

Activities	*% Time Spent Now*	*% Would Like to Spend*
1. Spouse/ Significant other		
2. Children		
3. Other family		
4. Work		
5. Personal time/ Recreation		
6. Exercise		
7. School/Education		
8. Sleep		
9. Friends		
10. Household/Yard, auto, and so forth		
11. Organizations/Clubs		
12. Other activities (specify):		

_____

_____

_____

_____

My plan to balance my lifestyle better is to _____

_____

_____

_____

APPENDIX F:
INVITATION TO MAINTENANCE
AND RELAPSE-PREVENTION SEMINARS

The Cognitive Therapy Program offers a seminar to help former patients of this program to maintain their progress and prevent relapse by continuing to use cognitive therapy skills on their own on a regular basis. In these seminars the principles of cognitive therapy are reviewed and methods of anticipating and preventing setbacks are explored. Many former patients have found these seminars to be helpful in maintaining their improved emotional health and in reinforcing their efforts to be their own therapists. The focus of these group seminars is educational and skill-building. It should be noted that these seminars are not a sub-stitute for ongoing individual or group therapy, but are intended to provide a "refresher" session for former participants in cognitive-behavioral therapy. These seminars are held every _____. You are invited to participate in the next seminar which will be held on _____ and will be led by _____. We feel that you will benefit from participation in this follow-up seminar. Please call _____ if you are interested in attending, or if you have any questions concerning this.

APPENDIX G:
POSSIBLE AGENDA FOR
MAINTENANCE AND RELAPSE-
PREVENTION SEMINAR

Brief Review

Review of participants' successes.
Review of cognitive-behavioral techniques.
Review of problem-solving skills.

Relapse-Prevention

Personal early warning signs of relapse.
Anticipating high-risk situations.
Coping with setbacks/Formulating an emergency plan.
Ways of using cognitive-behavior therapy in everyday life.

Topics Requested by Participants

Examples: Improving self-esteem.
            Time management.
            Effective decision-making.

Goal-Setting

Personal short-term goals.
Specific steps to achieve goals.
Possible obstacles to achieving goals.
Methods to overcome obstacles.

REFERENCES

Baker, A. L., & Wilson, P. H. (1985). Cognitive-behavior therapy for depression: The effects of booster sessions on relapse. *Behavior Therapy, 16,* 335-344.

Bandura, A. (1977). *Social Learning Theory.* Englewood Cliffs, NJ: Prentice Hall.

Barber, J. P., & DeRubeis, R. J. (1989). On second thoughts: Where the action is in cognitive therapy. *Cognitive Therapy and Research, 13,* 441-457.

Barlow, D. H., & Wolfe, B. E. (1981). Behavioral approaches to anxiety disorders: A report on the NIMH-SUNY Albany Research conference. *Journal of Consulting and Clinical Psychology, 49,* 448-454.

Beck, A. T. (1967). *Depression: Causes and Treatment.* Philadelphia: University of Pennsylvania Press.

Beck, A. T. (1976). *Cognitive Therapy and the Emotional Disorders.* New York: International Universities Press.

Beck, A. T., Brown, G., Epstein, N., & Steer, R. A. (1988). An inventory for measuring clinical anxiety: Psychometric properties. *Journal of Consulting and Clinical Psychology, 56,* 893-897.

Beck, A. T., & Emery, G. (1985). *Anxiety Disorders and Phobias: A Cognitive Perspective.* New York: Harper & Row.

Beck, A. T., & Freeman, A. A. (1990). *Cognitive Therapy of Personality Disorders.* New York: Guilford.

Beck, A. T., Rush, A. J., Shaw, B. F., & Emery, G. (1979). *Cognitive Therapy for Depression.* New York: Guilford.

Beck, A. T., Ward, C. H., Mendelson, M., Mock, J. E., & Erbaugh, J. (1961). An inventory for measuring depression. *Archives of General Psychiatry, 4,* 561-571.

Beck, J. S. (1994). *Cognitive Therapy: Basics and Beyond.* New York: Guilford.

Belsher, G., & Costello, C. G. (1988). Relapse after recovery from unipolar depression: A critical review. *Psychological Bulletin, 104,* 84-96.

Billings, A. G., & Moos, R. H. (1982). Psychosocial theory and research on depression: An integrative framework and review. *Clinical Psychology Review, 2,* 213-237.

Blackburn, I. M., Eunson, K. M., & Bishop, S. (1986). A two year naturalistic follow-up of depressed patients treated with cognitive therapy, pharmacotherapy and a combination of both. *Journal of Affective Disorders, 10,* 67-75.

Brown, G. W., & Harris, T. (1978). *Social Origins of Depression.* New York: The Free Press.

Brownell, K. D., Marlatt, G. A., Lichenstein, E., & Wilson, G. T. (1986). Understanding and preventing relapse. *American Psychologist, 4,* 765-782.

Burns, D. D. (1981). *Feeling Good.* New York: Signet.

Butler, G., Cullington, A., Hibbert, G., Klimes, I., & Gelder, M. (1987). Anxiety management for persistent generalized anxiety. *British Journal of Psychiatry, 151,* 535-542.

Chiauzzi, E. J. (1992). *Preventing Relapse in the Addictions: A Biopsychosocial Approach.* New York: Pergamon.

Clum, G. (1990). *Coping With Panic.* New York: Brooks-Cole.

Dattilio, F. M., & Padesky, C. A. (1990). *Cognitive Therapy With Couples.* Sarasota, FL: Professional Resource Exchange.

Eaves, G., & Rush, A. J. (1984). Cognitive patterns in symptomatic and remitted unipolar major depression. *Journal of Abnormal Psychology, 93,* 31-40.

Emmelkamp, P. M. J., & Kuipers, A. C. M. (1979). Agoraphobia: A follow-up study four years after treatment. *British Journal of Psychiatry, 128,* 86-89.

Epstein, N., Schlessinger, S., & Dryden, W. E. (1988). *Cognitive Behavior Therapy With Families.* New York: Brunner-Mazel.

Evans, M. D., Hollon, S. D., DeRubeis, R. J., Piasecki, J., Tuason, V. B., & Vye, C. (1985, November). *Accounting for Relapse in a Treatment Outcome Study of Depression.* Paper presented to the annual meeting of the Association for the Advancement of Behavior Therapy, Boston, MA.

Foa, E. B., Grayson, J. B., Steketee, G., Doppelt, H. C., Turner, R. M., & Lattimer, P. L. (1983). Success and failure in the behavioral treatment of obsessive-compulsives. *Journal of Consulting and Clinical Psychology, 15,* 287-297.

Frank, E., Kupfer, D. J., Wagner, E. F., McEachran, A. B., & Cornes, C. (1991). Efficacy of interpersonal psychotherapy as a maintenance treatment of recurrent depression: Contributing factors. *Archives of General Psychiatry, 48,* 1053-1058.

Fyer, A., Liebowitz, M., Gorman, J., Compeas, R., Levin, A., Davies, S., Goetz, D., & Klein, D. (1987). Discontinuation of alprazolam in panic patients. *American Journal of Psychiatry, 144,* 303-308.

Gonzales, L. R., Lewinsohn, P. M., & Clark, G. N. (1985). A longitudinal follow-up of unipolar depressives: An investigation of predictors of relapse. *Journal of Consulting and Clinical Psychology, 53,* 461-469.

Greenwald, M. A. (1988). Programming treatment generalization. In L. Michelson & M. Asher (Eds), *Handbook of Anxiety and Stress Disorders* (pp. 583-616). New York: Plenum.

Guidano, V. F., & Liotti, G. (1983). *Cognitive Processes and Emotional Disorders: A Structural Approach to Psychotherapy.* New York: Guilford.

Holcomb, W. R. (1986). Stress innoculation therapy with anxiety and stress disorders of acute psychiatric inpatients. *Journal of Clinical Psychology, 42,* 864-872.

Hollon, S. D., & Najavits, L. (1988). Review of empirical studies of cognitive therapy. In A. J. Rush & A. T. Beck (Eds), *American Psychiatric Association Review of Psychiatry: Cognitive Therapy* (Vol. 7, pp. 643-666). Washington, DC: American Psychiatric Press.

Holmes, T. H., & Rahe, R. H. (1967). The Social Readjustment Scale. *Journal of Psychosomatic Research, 11,* 213-218.

Kanner, A. D., Coyne, J. C., Schaefer, C., & Lazurus, R. S. (1987). Comparison of two modes of stress measurement: Daily hassles and uplifts versus life events. *Journal of Behavioral Medicine, 4,* 24-29.

Klerman, G. L. (1978). Long term maintenance of affective disorders. In C. Lipton, A. Dimascio, & K. Killam (Eds), *Psychopharmacology: A Generation of Progress* (pp. 1303-1311). New York: Raven Press.

Klerman, G. L., Weissman, M. M., Rounsaville, B., & Chevron, E. (1984). *Interpersonal Psychotherapy of Depression.* New York: Basic Books.

Kovacs, M., Rush, A. J., Beck, A. T., & Hollon, S. D. (1981). Depressed outpatients treated with cognitive therapy or pharmacotherapy. *Archives of General Psychiatry, 38,* 33-39.

Krantz, S. E. (1987). A tip on relapse prevention. *International Cognitive Therapy Newsletter, 3*(1), 1.

Krantz, S. E., Hill, R. D., Foster-Rawlings, S., & Zeeve, C. (1984). Therapist's use of and perceptions of strategies for maintenance and generalization. *The Cognitive Behaviorist, 6,* 19-22.

Lazurus, A. A., & Fay, A. (1984). Some strategies for promoting generalization and maintenance. *The Cognitive Behaviorist, 6,* 7-9.

Lewinsohn, P. M., & Graf, M. (1973). Pleasant activities and depression. *Journal of Consulting and Clinical Psychology, 41,* 261-268.

Lewinsohn, P. M., Munoz, R. F., Youngren, M. A., & Zeiss, A. M. (1978). *Control Your Depression.* Englewood Cliffs, NJ: Prentice Hall.

Lewinsohn, P. M., Sullivan, J. M., & Grossup, S. J. (1982). Behavioral therapy: Clinical applications. In A. J. Rush (Ed.), *Short-Term Psychotherapies for the Depressed Patient* (pp. 50-87). New York: Guilford.

Ludgate, J. W. (1991). *The Long Term Effectiveness of Cognitive Therapy in the Treatment of Depression: A Five-Year Follow Up Study of Treated Patients.* Unpublished doctoral dissertation, University of Dublin, Ireland.

Ludgate, J. W. (1994). Cognitive behavior therapy and depressive relapse: Justified optimism or unwarranted complacency? *Behavioral and Cognitive Psychotherapy, 22*(1), 1-12.

Ludgate, J. W., Reinecke, M. A., & Beck, A. T. (1987, November). *Cognitive Vulnerability and Outcome in Depression: The Dysfunctional Attitude Scale as a Predictor of Relapse After Psychotherapy.* Paper presented at the annual meeting of the Association for the Advancement of Behavior Therapy, Boston, MA.

Marlatt, G. A., & Gordon, S. J. (Eds.). (1985). *Relapse Prevention.* New York: Guilford.

McKay, M. D., & Fanning, P. (1991). *Prisoners of Belief.* Oakland, CA: New Harbinger Press.

Meichenbaum, D. (1977). *Stress Inoculation.* New York: Pergamon.

Meyer, V., Levy, R., & Schnurer, A. (1974). The behavioral treatment of obsessive compulsive disorder. In H. R. Beech (Ed.), *Obsessional States* (pp. 233-258). London: Methuen.

Michelson, L. K., & Marchione, K. (1991). Behavioral, cognitive and pharmacological treatments of panic disorder with agoraphobia: Critique and synthesis. *Journal of Consulting and Clinical Psychology, 59,* 100-114.

Miller, I. W. (1984). Strategies for maintenance of treatment gains for depressed patients. *The Cognitive Behaviorist, 6,* 10-13.

Mines, R. A., & Merrill, C. A. (1987). Bulimia: Cognitive behavioral treatment and relapse prevention. *Journal of Counseling and Development, 65,* 562-564.

Munby, J., & Johnston, D. W. (1980). Agoraphobia: The long-term follow up of behavioral treatment. *British Journal of Psychiatry, 137,* 408-427.

Munroe, S. M., & Wade, S. L. (1988). Life events. In C. G. Last & M. Hersen (Eds.), *Handbook of Anxiety Disorders* (pp. 293-305). New York: Pergamon.

Persons, J. B. (1989). *Cognitive Therapy in Practice: A Case Formulation Approach.* New York: W. W. Norton.

Persons, J. B., Burns, D. D., & Parloff, J. M. (1988). Predictors of drop out and outcome in cognitive therapy for depression in a private practice setting. *Cognitive Therapy and Research, 12,* 287-300.

Rapee, R. M. (1991). Generalized Anxiety Disorder: A review of clinical features and theoretical concepts. *Clinical Psychology Review, 111,* 419-440.

Salkovskis, P. M., Jones, D. R. O., & Clark, D. M. (1986). Respiratory control in the treatment of panic attacks: Replication and extension with concurrent measurement of behavior and PCO2. *British Journal of Psychiatry, 148,* 526-532.

Shiffman, S. (1992). Relapse process and relapse prevention in the addictive behaviors. *The Behavior Therapist, 15,* 9-11.

Simons, A. D., Murphy, G. E., Levine, J. L., & Wetzel, R. D. (1986). Cognitive therapy and pharmacotherapy of depression: Sustained improvement over 1 year. *Archives of General Psychiatry, 43,* 43-48.

Speilberger, C. D. (1983). *Manual for the State-Trait Anxiety Inventory.* Palo Alto, CA: Consulting Psychologists Press.

Tearnan, B. H., Telch, M. J., & Keefe, P. (1984). Etiology and onset of agoraphobia: A critical review. *Comprehensive Psychiatry, 25,* 511-562.

Teasdale, J. D. (1985). Psychological treatments for depression. How do they work? *Behavior Research and Therapy, 23,* 157-165.

Telch, M. J., Tearnan, B. H., & Taylor, C. B. (1983). Antidepressant medication in the treatment of agoraphobia: A critical review. *Behavior Research and Therapy, 21,* 505-527.

Thompson, L. W., Gallagher, D., & Czirr, R. (1988). Personality disorder and outcome in the treatment of later life depression. *Journal of Geriatric Psychiatry and Neurology, 121,* 133-146.

Turner, R. M. (1987). The effects of personality disorder on the outcome of social anxiety reduction. *Journal of Personality Disorders, 1,* 136-146.

Weissman, M. M., Klerman, G. L., Paykel, E. S., Pruscoff, A., & Hanson, B. (1974). Treatment effects on the social adjustment of depressed patients. *Archives of General Psychiatry, 30,* 771-778.

Weissman, M. M., Klerman, G. L., Pruscoff, B. A., Sholomkas, D., & Padian, N. (1981). Depressed outpatients: Results one

year after treatment with drugs and/or interpersonal psychotherapy. *Archives of General Psychiatry, 38,* 51-55.

Young, J. E. (1994). *Cognitive Therapy for Personality Disorders: A Schema-Focused Approach* (rev. ed.). Sarasota, FL:
Professional Resource Press.

Zitrin, C. M., Klein, D. F., & Woerner, M. G. (1980). Treatment
of agoraphobia with group exposure in vivo and Imipramine.
Archives of General Psychiatry, 37, 63-72.